YOU ARE ENOUGH

Heal From Past Hurts & Reclaim Your Power and Identity

Katina Horton

Illinois

YOU ARE ENOUGH,

Copyright © 2021, Katina Horton-Valley of Grace Ministries. All Rights Reserved.

Jacket Cover design by Katina Horton

Jacket Cover photograph by Jody Lynn Photography

Jacket Cover Images – Canva stock images

Printed in the United States of America

No portion of this book can be reproduced, stored, or transmitted in any form or by any means, unless cited and quoted as a source for research purposes or in printed reviews, without the prior written permission of Katina Horton-Valley of Grace Ministries. If you would like permission, please contact katinahorton@thevalleyofgrace.com.

https://thevalleyofgrace.com

ISBN: 978-0-578314-37-2 (hardcover)

3

This book is dedicated to all the warrior women in toxic relationships who have signed up to do the courageous work of healing and getting their power and identity back.

When you heal, you become empowered. And when you become empowered, you impact your home, community, nation, and society in general.

"And Moses built an altar and called the name of it, The LORD Is My Banner."

Exodus 17:15, KJV

If this book has added value to your life, please kindly leave a review.

Table of Contents

Contents

Why the Transformation? 11
Healing and All of Its Many Flavors 33
We're Under Construction Now! 49
Healing After Past Hurts 59
Healing After Divorce 63
What Happens After You Leave? 91
Build Resilience and Flourish 107
Healing After Job, Church, and Family Hurt 131
Obstacles to Healing 151
How Shame Reenforces Trauma 175
The Thorn and The Gift 185
The Need for a Poison Container 195
Create An Empowered New Chapter of Life 207
Identity, Self-Worth, & Boundaries 209
Creating New Software 217
Acknowledgments 227
ABOUT THE AUTHOR 231

This book was Holy Spirit inspired by my experiences. And it is for educational purposes. It is not intended to be used to self-diagnose. I coach women in toxic relationships who seek to reclaim their power and identity so they will know they are enough. I am not a licensed therapist or clinician. If you are in serious trouble, please consult a licensed therapist.

Why the Transformation?

Watching a transformation show is exciting. Especially the ones where the ladies get a complete makeover. This complete makeover entails new hairstyle, makeup, and clothes.

The clothing budget is normally about two thousand dollars. Once the woman is ready to shop, she usually goes to several different high-end stores with the host of the show. It is at this point that she tries on several outfits.

Nine times out of ten, the host encourages her to buy a five- or six-hundred-dollar blazer, as well as a two-hundred-dollar pair of shoes. The shoes usually accompany another five or six hundred dollars on a leather purse or briefcase.

This is supposed to be the grand transformation.

If only life was that simple. Think about it, if all we had to do to be transformed was to buy new makeup, clothing, and hairstyles to change our lives, everybody would be doing it.

Unfortunately, that's not how it works. Transformation begins on the inside and moves outward.

Romans 12: 1-2 says: "Therefore, I urge you, brothers and sisters, in view of God's mercy, to offer your bodies as a living sacrifice, holy and pleasing to God—this is your true and proper worship. Do not conform to the pattern of this world, but be transformed by the renewing of your mind. Then you will be able to test and approve what God's will is—his good, pleasing and perfect will." (NIV)

The world's view of transformation is to change the outside so that you feel better. God's view of transformation is to get to the heart of the matter so you can heal better. In other words, you are going from the inside out by renewing your mind, and the transformation that takes place is an inevitable result of the inner work.

I want you to take a minute and go to another time and place.

You are going back to the time when you were a little girl. Picture yourself riding your bike, carefree with the wind blowing in your face.

If being a bike rider was not your thing, and the playground was, then picture hanging out with your neighborhood friends on the playground and swinging freely from the monkey bars.

Or maybe your spot was the beach. You are playing with your friends and using your favorite kit that your mother bought you. I am quite sure you know which one I am talking about. It is the hard plastic beach kit with the shovel that all the parents bought their kids back in the day.

You feel the sand in between your toes. You feel the sun and wind and freedom hitting your face. And guess what? You want to stay in this place forever.

The little girl inside of you is standing tall and saying, "I am enough".

Now, picture a short time later. You are outside with nine other girls, and about to play a game. Since there are ten of you, you will have two teams of even numbers. The team leaders have already been picked.

The pretty girls were always the ones that were selected as the team leaders.

Pretty soon, the leaders are starting to select their team members. As you are anxiously waiting to hear news of which team you will be on, you hear other team members making comments that are supposed to be whispers, but they are not. "Don't pick her. She's not light enough." Someone else says, "Don't pick her. She's not fast enough." Someone else says, "Don't pick her. She's not pretty enough."

The death words go on and on. You feel the weight of them, reaching way down into the depths of your soul.

Finally, one of the team leaders says, "Okay, well, I guess you can join our team." You are relieved to have been picked. But it's too late.

The internal damage of what has transpired proved to be too much for your soul. You are standing, ready to play, but deep down in the depths of your soul, you are sitting down. And there is not enough freedom in the world to change your posture.

As you are reading these words, I can hear you saying, "Oh no, that's not me."

Oh, but yes, it is. Somehow, somewhere, and at some point, in time, someone told you something that crushed your soul.

Not only did it crush your soul, but it also made the little girl inside of you sit down. You are standing on the outside, but you are sitting down within.

And guess what? It was only a few words that they said. Those few words have been the foundation of your brokenness that has been leading you all these years.

You are cowering in the hallway, hiding in the shadows, in the back of the church, behind all the other women in your small group.

At the time of your pain, you put on a banner that said, "I am not enough".

Or maybe your banner said something like this:

"I am not pretty enough."

"I am not light enough."

"I am not dark enough."

"I am not skinny enough."

"I am not sophisticated enough."

"I am not smart enough."

"I am not fashionable enough."

"I am not black enough."

"I am not white enough."

Whatever it said, it has a problem attached to it: you never took it off.

In my memoir, "The Journey", I tell my complete story. However, for the purposes of this book, I will reference a few snapshots to assist you in your reclamation process.

When I was eleven years old, my mom and I entered the apartment that we knew as home. To our surprise, almost the entire apartment was cleaned out except for the kitchen set and my parents' bedroom furniture. To say that we stood there in shock is an understatement.

My mother's response to our revelation was, "Well, I guess your dad left."

At the time, I was devastated. But I didn't know how to put that devastation into words.

Putting it into words looked like being jealous when my other friends were spending time with their fathers, when I did not know what to do with the absence of mine.

Don't get me wrong. Their split was necessary. The abuse that I witnessed in my home was more than enough proof of that. It being done in this manner was a whole 'nother level.

The hardest thing for a child to reconcile within themselves is the byproduct of separation and/or divorce. There are some relationships that are stronger than ever when the parents are no longer together. And then there are other relationships that end up being estranged, leaving footprints on your mind, body, and soul.

Our parents are not perfect. And neither are we. They will disappoint us. And in turn, we will disappoint them. But one thing is for sure. We have to move on and live our lives.

Living our lives means not hopping on the "would have, could have, should have" ship, as I like to call it.

That ship has already left the port. And our unwillingness to face that fact alone is what will keep us standing there, and hoping and wishing that somehow it will return, allowing us to rewrite or revise our story.

It involves moving forward. We think we are moving forward. However, our perception and our reality become two totally different things.

After my dad left, I became married to the spirit of abandonment, loneliness, and rejection. I switched out my banner that said, "Loved as a Child of God" to one that read nice and loud, "I AM NOT ENOUGH".

I began to suffer from all kinds of insecurities, low self-esteem, and low self-worth. Everyone always complimented my mother on how beautiful she looked. And I would one hundred percent agree.

However, when you hear a thirteen-year-old teenage girl tell another teenage girl outside of the church doors, "Her mother is so beautiful. I wonder what happened to her?", your banner gets a little bit longer, wrapping around to your backside.

Instead of just wearing, "I AM NOT ENOUGH" by itself, I added two others, walking across the stage like Miss America shouting: "I AM NOT PRETTY ENOUGH" and "I AM NOT DARK ENOUGH".

Why dark enough? My mother is dark, and so, in my teenage mind, I had to be darker in order to be accepted as being enough. The enemy coupled with my own childlike imaginations needed to have a way to make sense of everything that did not seem right in the world, and more importantly, in my life.

I started competing in spelling bees and oratorical competitions as a child. And towards the latter end of my grammar school adventure, I ranked pretty high. So, when I saw my Dad every few years, and he said, "Baby, you put Donoghue on the map!", that's when I knew I was enough.

I equated enoughness with performance, but it still did not change the fact that the little girl inside of me was sitting down.

Still wearing that banner, I got hooked up in a few dating relationships that challenged my worthiness. The last of these relationships was with my ex-husband. After getting married, it did not take long for me to realize every broken area in him exploited every broken area in me.

In my brokenness I thought that I could fix/change/control him and the situation so I could have my needs met, and at the same time, eliminate the emotionally abusive behavior that I was receiving. I burned the midnight oil to find a solution.

What I failed to realize early on is that I had hooked up with someone whose brokenness reenforced my not enoughness. And in his brokenness, his unspoken message to me became, "I am everything that you are not."

This unspoken message damaged my soul. I walked around thinking that because of my personal appearance, I did not deserve better treatment. That I should just be happy with him, because I was not going to find another medium-brown-eyed handsome guy.

The devil has all kinds of ways to keep us entangled in his web.

My self-worth was riding on my ex-husband. Like Leah going after Jacob in the bible, I needed him to make me enough. And little did I know, he could not solve that problem for me. Only Jesus could.

When it got to the point of me entering a state of languishing, I ran after my ex-husband like my life depended on it. The more I ran after him, the more he ran away from me. It was like a game of cat and mouse.

I thought that all I had to do was to come up with the magic formula, and we could get back to the beginning. Boy, was I wrong! All the magic formulas in the world could not fix us. We needed a serious "come to Jesus moment".

God was not going to stop me from chasing him. And he wasn't going to stop him from putting me down. In his gracious love, he was not going to go against our free will.

A lot of times, we think to ourselves, "Why in the world would a loving God allow this?" And at the same time, he is thinking, "Why not?"

What does John 3:16 tell us?

"For God so loved the world, that he gave his only begotten Son, that whosoever believeth in him should not perish, but have everlasting life." (KJV)

Think about this. God gave us a gift of love. And when we are given a gift, we do not have to pay for it. And there is something else that happens. We do not have to accept it either.

A person can hold out the gift that they have for us, and, in turn, we can say, "No, thank you. I don't want it."

Salvation is that such gift. Love is that gift. Free will is that gift. If God forced us to accept his gift of salvation, then it would mean that love could no longer be love. For love to exist, love has to have freedom.

God does not go around controlling us like puppets. He wants us free, healed, and living abundant lives. However, in his compassion and grace, he says, *The choice is yours, Baby.*

Through the power of the Holy Spirit, along with me being in a desperate state of languishing, I made the choice to walk into a therapist's office. When I walked into my therapist's office, I was exhausted, carrying a huge backpack of perfectionism. Instead of wearing Luke 10:27 as my mantra, I wore "I'm not enough" on my sleeves, in my heart, in my mind, and in my soul.

After three intense sessions, my therapist suggested, "What do you think about a three-month in-house separation?" To be honest, what I really thought was, "There's no way I want that. I just have to figure out the magic formula." And I believe she could sense the hesitation in my voice because her response reflected that.

She stated that our agreement of in-house separation was contingent upon both of us being in individual therapy. We agreed to her terms. And as God would have it, that separation was my HUGE "Be still and know" moment that the angels in heaven were singing about. That was the moment that completely changed my life.

No more chasing after him. No more begging him. No more trying to fix him or the relationship. No more trying to force him to go against his free will that he was given by God.

Because guess what? Love involves freedom.

Change happens the moment we release the grip on control, and grab onto the rope, holding on for dear life, placing our eyes, ears, soul, and mind on Jesus, who is the author and finisher of our faith.

I began my journey of healing, empowerment, and reclamation of my power and identity. It wasn't an easy journey. My car hit a lot of bumps in the road. But it was the best thing I could have ever done.

As you read part of my story, you were probably thinking to yourself, "Oh, man! I'm glad that wasn't me. By the grace of God, she made it."

That's where I beg to differ.

Like the Windows operating system, we all have a desktop where the "I am not (_____) enough" occurred. My background wallpaper was the empty living room that I walked into. And your background wallpaper will look different. The important thing to remember is: we all have one.

And although your story is not an exact replica of my story, you still have a story. And, somewhere along the way, the unhealed little girl that is deep inside of you was never able to stand up again because of that story.

Acknowledging the truth is the beginning of transforming your life. To snatch off your beauty pageant banner that you have worn for so long would bring freedom. And along with that freedom comes responsibility.

Sister, Queen, Daughter of God, you have work to do.

God sits on the sidelines for each one of us, cheering us on and saying, "Be ye transformed by the renewing of your mind." (Romans 12:2)

I can hear your response right now. "Well, I hear what you are saying, but I still don't believe that little girl exists in my life."

She exists every time you find yourself going from one toxic relationship to the next. And it's not just romantic. That's just the beginning. They are also your friends, coworkers, ministry partners, sisters and brothers in Christ, and family members.

We know that the little girl exists when you have been hurt and left in a state of languishing, and then within six months, you are right back on the relationship scene with a new guy.

No time for healing. No time for reflecting. No "Come to Jesus" moment. Nothing.

We know that little girl exists when therein lies a disconnect between saying our daily affirmations, mantras, and decrees, and knowing that our heart and soul wounds are screaming out for air because we have continued to place a Band-Aid on them.

We know that she exists when we bleed out on others, making them our poison container a.k.a. punching bag.

We know she exists when our past hurts become our operating system, with each hurt running in the foreground, hogging up memory instead of as a background process.

We know that little girl exists when we compare ourselves to other women like the craziness that went on with Jacob's daughters, Rachel, and Leah, thinking that the other woman is the problem, but our real issue is with God.

We all want what the other woman has, but what we do not want is the journey that is attached to the "success". To whom much is given, much is required. But we forget about that part, don't we?

And lastly, we know she exists when we normalize abuse and soul ties like we're going grocery shopping, instead of realizing that there is a serious problem going on inside.

BUT GOD is always on the sidelines rooting for every single one of us.

Okay Katina! I have heard enough. What do I need to do?

You need to heal. In order for you to reclaim your power and identity, healing is the first thing on the menu. We cannot go to the restaurant and order any more daily affirmations and mantras until we have had the healing portion first.

Healing and All of Its Many Flavors

Healing sounds good and all, but you need a breakdown of exactly what it is. You can't do something without knowing what that something means and/or entails.

Healing is going through the emotional, mental, physical, and spiritual process of turning your wounds into scars. A wound is the open emotional, mental, physical, and spiritual evidence that you have been hurt, and are currently bleeding out from that hurt.

A scar is the closed emotional, mental, physical, and spiritual evidence that you have been hurt, but are no longer affected by or bleeding out from that hurt because you have gone through an extensive process of not allowing that past hurt to control your life.

Having scars means that your past hurts are no longer your operating system. How will you know? The scripture tells us "For out of the abundance of the heart the mouth speaketh." (Matthew 12:34, KJV)

If you are not aware of what is coming out of your mouth, record yourself several times a day as you freely move about your house. If you have children, be honest and ask them if there are things that you are saying to them that is hurtful. And then, ask a few trusted friends and coworkers.

You also want to be prepared for what they say. It may not feel good to hear that your words have brought death unto others. However, this new knowledge is for the intention of healing, learning, growing, and reclaiming your power and identity.

We as women devalue ourselves all the time. We say things to ourselves that we would never say to another woman. Or if we do, it is not as harsh.

And, as my therapist helped me to realize when I was going through my journey of healing, we project what is going on with us onto other people. Devaluing ourselves causes the death words we have spoken to go into the depths of our minds, bodies, and souls. The cells in our bodies are taking notes as if they are in a college lecture class.

Just like the book, The Body Keeps the Score" by Bessel Van Der Kolk tells us, our bodies know what's going on way before our minds catch wind of it. Here is an example: I was watching a popular television show. The storyline and acting were good. The culture displayed in the movie reminded me of home.

I had to stop watching it after about fifteen minutes. They said one curse word so many times that my body was literally aching. I couldn't believe it.

We forget our belongings at home. Next thing you know, we are asking ourselves, "How could you have been so_____?" All the while, our cells are taking notes, so our bodies, minds, and souls remember we are _____.

The truth of the matter is, we are all human. We are going to make mistakes. Some of those mistakes are going to be hot mess mistakes. But, we are going to make them. On this side of heaven. Until Jesus returns. But we don't want our mistakes to become our life mantra.

Our mouths a.k.a., the sound cards of our hearts, also tell us what we think about other women we are in relationship with on a daily basis. If we are not careful, we can easily end up judging and criticizing their men, hair, weight, outfits, cars, homes, you name it.

God's desire is that each one of us live according to the abundant life that he has promised. Healing our wounds means being cautious and protecting our wounds. The last thing we want to do is to catch other people's infections. But we also don't want to hand out any.

Think about this: Your child has cut up their knee pretty badly. You put a BAND-AID on it. The initial shock has worn off and they have finally stopped crying.

You have a decision to make. Do you tell your child who has shorts on to go outside, and wallow around in the dirt again just because they have a BAND-AID on? No, you would not.

Why? Because you know that once playtime gets good, they will put their knees in the mud, forget about being careful, and it's only a matter of time before the BAND-AID is coming off.

After the BAND-AID falls off, all the dirt, and whatever is in that dirt is going to get inside of that open wound. And before you know it, you will be taking your child to the pediatrician to assess the damage and get some serious antibiotics so that the infection doesn't go septic.

This is the same way it goes in our personal lives. We are bleeding wide open after just leaving a toxic relationship, and then we listen to our girlfriends say something like, "Girl, you should go ahead and date. You got one life to live. What's the point in waiting? You're not getting any younger. Tomorrow is not promised."

You take the bait, and then the next thing you know, your system goes septic. Instead of you just having trauma like before, this new man has given you full blown PTSD, and you are left with the hard reality of trying to figure out how you are going to recover.

Like with anything, there has to be balance. Too much air on a physical wound, and we risk infection. Too much time with a BAND-AID on a physical wound without adequate air, and we also risk infection. My grandmother had a saying for this kind of situation. I think you know what that saying is, but I won't say it here.

It is tempting to think that God does not care about our problems. But he does. Every. Single. One. Of. Them. If he knows and cares about every single strand of hair on our heads, he knows and cares about every single one of our heartaches.

In his word, he tells us: "He is the healer of the brokenhearted. He is the one who bandages their wounds." (Psalms 147:3, GW)

One thing about healing is that it is of necessity that we have the right kind of environment. As the experts tell us, the five people that we hang around the most are the ones who are the most influential in our lives. If those five people are bleeding out all the time, then we are the jar that they are pouring into.

A person with alcohol and drug addictions can't expect to heal if they continue to hang out with alcohol and drug addicts. A person with shopping addictions can't hang out with friends who go to department stores all the time.

And last, but not least, a person who has just come out of their fifth toxic relationship cannot hang out with other toxic people and think that they will be okay. It just does not work that way.

God wants us completely healed. He doesn't want us playing around in Egypt, thinking that nothing is going to happen. He wants us to get to the Promised Land. It is the land that is flowing with milk and honey, not void of problems, but filled with empowerment, resilience, and flourishing.

Parts of us will need to heal with others, and other parts of us will need to heal in solitude. I like to think of this solitude as the "Be still and know" moment.

The "be still and know moment" can be a moment once you are healed. However, if you are not, and you are in a toxic relationship, or just left a toxic relationship for example, a "be still and know moment" could be six months to three years, or even longer. It is where we heal, gain clarity, perspective, and empowerment to reach new levels. If you are unable to stop chasing the other person in the toxic relationship, you are not ready for healing.

In Psalms 46:10, when God said, "Be still", he was not trying to keep something away from us. He was trying to give something away to us. He literally meant, "stop moving". Somehow, as women, we equate that with "try to fix it/figure it out on your own". That's not what God meant.

The second part says, "and know". To know something or someone, is to spend time with them. To know God is to spend time with him just like we spend time with our family, friends, coworkers, and ministry partners. The "I am God" part reminds us that he is sovereign. He loves us and wants the best for us. He is in control, and we are not.

If we are not balancing out being with the crowd, and learning to be alone, we can easily feel tempted to go back to the crowd or the man to fill us with what only God can give us.

None of our brokenness is too far away from God. We just have to call out to him, trust him, and trust the process. As Christians, we often forget that we have a role to play in our healing process.

Look at the man at the pool of Bethesda. He was in his state for thirty-eight years. Jesus healed him.

Then, he told the man to pick up his bed and walk. He did not say, "Let me pick up your bed for you."

We have a responsibility to do our part. God does his part by giving us the promises in his word, along with being there with us in the fire. He did not promise us that we would be walking on beds of Eden.

"The thief comes only to steal and kill and destroy; I have come that they may have life, and have it to the full." (John 10:10, NIV)

Our part entails doing the messy but rewarding work.

God is not going to call our therapist, coach, support group, etc. He is not going to journal for us or release our emotions. But guess what? He is going to walk through every single part of the journey with us.

He is going to walk through the fire with us. He did with Shadrach, Meshach, and Abednego. And he is not about to stop doing it now.

"But now, this is what the L*ORD* *says—*

   he who created you, Jacob,

   he who formed you, Israel:

"Do not fear, for I have redeemed you;

   I have summoned you by name; you are mine.

When you pass through the waters,

   I will be with you;

and when you pass through the rivers,

   they will not sweep over you.

When you walk through the fire,

   you will not be burned;

   the flames will not set you ablaze.

(Isaiah 43:1-2, NIV)

There is no magic potion for healing a broken heart. Each one of us will have a different process. The important thing to remember is that we can't skip over any of the parts.

The second thing of importance next to understanding the necessity of having a "be still and know moment" when it comes to healing is owning our stories. When we own our stories, we own our healing. When we disown our stories, we disown our healing.

We all wish that the contents of our book were just a tad bit different than reality. But remember, we can't rewrite or revise our story. We can only move forward and write new chapters.

Like in a fairytale, we may have adopted other people as our family of origin other than our biological family. There is nothing wrong with adopting spiritual friends and other sisters and brothers in Christ as our family.

Adopting them as our spiritual family and using them to replace our family of origin is two different things. Replacing your family of origin is being in denial. And if you refuse to own your family of origin, it means that you are not ready to heal because you have to go back to the issues that existed with them.

The next important thing to remember when it comes to healing is that we have to feel in order to heal. Feeling means being curious enough to allow our emotions to bring the informational memories to mind so that we can start dissecting some of what has held us in bondage for so long.

Feeling also helps us get to the root of our unusual behaviors. A lot of times, the unusual behaviors exist because we are not feeling.

It took a while for me to be able to connect the fact that some of my behaviors, such as picking and peeling my skin, along with having trichotillomania, that started in childhood were related to trauma, and the fact that I was not allowing myself to feel my emotions so I could heal. I did not have a toolbox for regulating my emotions, and thus, the behavior took its place.

If you are ready to reclaim your power and identity, rip off that "I AM NOT ENOUGH" banner, and let's get started.

48

We're Under Construction Now!

When we heal, we go under construction. Think about driving for instance. When you have the construction workers fixing the streets, highways, etc., you have to take the construction (detour) route.

The construction route is extremely inconvenient.

It is the same thing with healing. The end result for both situations is that the path is less bumpy. It does not mean that you won't have to do a little bit more construction (healing) on that road later on. It means that the foundation (operating system) with which you are driving with is not called "past hurts".

Some of us refuse to go under construction. When we refuse to go under construction, we end up with what I call alternative construction healing. We feel that we are entitled to do things the way that we want to do them, and the end result of that entitlement is that we end up back at home.

Case and point: you leave your house headed to the grocery store. The path that you normally take is under construction. You see the cones leading you to a different route to go to the grocery store.

In your mind, you say, "Ain't nobody got time for this!" You go the way that you always go. And guess what? The old way leads you right back to your house.

That's what happens when you skip over the steps of healing because you feel you should only have to do what you want to do. You end up back at home. It's kind of like playing a board game, and then you are getting pumped up because you know after the current player finishes his turn, you are going to win the game. Except you don't.

Just when you are ready to pounce on everyone and win the game, you are sent back home with a "See ya, wouldn't want to be ya!" Not fun at all. But it is what happens when you choose alternative construction healing. You return right to the point where you started out: on "E" for empty.

Pit stop healing works a little bit differently, although the end result is just the same. Say for instance, you put five dollars' worth of gas in your car instead of filling it up. And trust me, sometimes you only have five dollars to your name, and I understand that because I have been there and done that so many times where I have lost count.

For all intent and purposes in this example, we are talking about being able to afford the gas but refusing to fill up.

So, the next thing you know, you are literally stranded out in the middle of nowhere. You call emergency roadside assistance for gas. They give you just enough gas to make it to the gas station.

When you get there, you put another five dollars in the tank. And before you know it, you are stranded once again. Then, you pick up the phone and call for emergency roadside assistance.

It does not make sense to keep doing this. But we do it. We want what we want. And no one can tell us otherwise.

You go to therapy for an issue (death, divorce, job loss, etc.) that is going on, and you get a pit stop (five dollar fill up) healing special when you really need a full tank.

Several more life traumas occur. You go to therapy for a pit stop for each of those issues. Each time you finish therapy, you are back to running on "E".

You never took the time to get to the root of the problem of your not enoughness. The shortcuts turned into longcuts, as I like to call it. So, in essence, you feel like you never made progress.

To fill up with a full tank of gas is to go back to the very beginning. The beginning being your childhood and moving forward to today. It might sound like a lot of work. And it is. I'm not going to lie to you. But I'm not sugarcoating it either. Running on empty is a lot of work too. However, you haven't figured that out yet.

People who know me know my saying, "When you don't have all the tools you need, you start off at a negative."

Mephibosheth was Jonathan's son. David wanted to make sure that he took care of anyone that was left in Saul's household. Basically, he wanted to give them the hookup. He found out from a conversation with one of Saul's stewards that Jonathan's son, Mephibosheth, was alive and residing in Lo Debar.

David immediately had Mephibosheth brought to him so he could reap the benefits of his table. Here are the scripture verses stating how this played out:

"So King David had him brought from Lo Debar, from the house of Makir son of Ammiel.

When Mephibosheth son of Jonathan, the son of Saul, came to David, he bowed down to pay him honor.

David said, "Mephibosheth!"

"At your service," he replied. "Don't be afraid," David said to him, "for I will surely show you kindness for the sake of your father Jonathan. I will restore to you all

the land that belonged to your grandfather Saul, and you will always eat at my table."

Mephibosheth bowed down and said, "What is your servant, that you should notice a dead dog like me?"

Then the king summoned Ziba, Saul's steward, and said to him, "I have given your master's grandson everything that belonged to Saul and his family.

You and your sons and your servants are to farm the land for him and bring in the crops, so that your master's grandson may be provided for. And Mephibosheth, grandson of your master, will always eat at my table." (Now Ziba had fifteen sons and twenty servants.)" (2 Samuel 9:5-10, NIV)

Mephibosheth called himself a dead dog. To call yourself that, you must believe that you are the lowest of the low. So, in essence, Mephibosheth lived off the banner that we all find ourselves living off: "I

AM NOT ENOUGH!" Bottom line: He didn't believe that he was worthy.

Where did this come from? We have to go back to the beginning. Earlier in 2 Samuel, we are told that when Mephibosheth was five years old, as soon as the nurse found out about Jonathan and Saul's death, she grabbed Mephibosheth to mount the horse, and he fell. This incident made him lame in his feet.

I'm quite sure that his physical limitations led to some taunting by other children, and then society in general if he got to the place of calling himself a dead dog. When something is dead, there is no use for them.

After his accident, someone told him that he was not enough. And he believed the lie. All those years!

This whole story reminds me of God's love for us. Initially, we were unworthy because of our sin. The payment for our sins is death.

However, Jesus' death on the cross redeemed us, making us worthy as sons and daughters of God. This worthiness and identity qualify us to sit at the table with God in heavenly places. Just like Mephibosheth at the physical table of David the king.

The truth is, we walk around unaware of this very fact.

"For he raised us from the dead along with Christ and seated us with him in the heavenly realms because we are united with Christ Jesus."

(Ephesians 2:6, NLT)

Healing After Past Hurts

Past hurts include, but are not limited to, childhood wounds, your own brokenness, and other relationships that wounded you. When we heal, it does not mean that those issues may never come to mind again. We are human, and part of being human involves remembering both the good and bad.

It helps us in making future choices, especially when it comes to choosing a new mate. It does not mean we are dwelling on the past hurt.

Healing is a lifelong journey. So, when I speak of healing from past hurts, I speak of it in terms of not having that particular issue running your whole life. They do not interrupt your everyday flow of life and hinder abundant living in general.

There are some people who think if you never cry about your hurts, it means that you are healed. I beg to differ. Some of us are more emotional than others. Crying should be part of the joy and sorrow that's expressed.

We are all wired up differently. So, I don't believe that crying over something that you have been through is a judge of how far you have come in healing. However, if you are trying to date someone new, and you have been crying for three hours a day every day, that would be a good indication of the fact that you are not ready yet.

One thing to remember is that when it comes to healing, you will be pulling back layers for years. But pulling back these layers means that we are able to mature and grow in the process. And when we are healing from past hurts, it brings resilience and perspective that we could not have gained any other way.

When I think of being healed enough to step into new relationships, I think of being able to walk around without bleeding all over the place. You are still doing the internal work. However, the internal work is not impeding your relationships. Your pain is contained.

Think about a bottle of pills. What kind of sense would it make to take that bottle of pills and pour it all over the floor in every room of the house so people could step on them? Same way with healing. When we bleed out, we give everybody and their momma bits and pieces of our emotional and mental problems. We know we are healed enough when our problems are contained in a bottle just like those pills. The last thing we want to do is to get stepped on.

Healing After Divorce

One of the main questions that women ask is, "How will I know when I am healed after a divorce?" There is no set time frame or clear set of rules for knowing how. However, there are a lot of things to take into consideration before thinking about taking such a big step.

I went to a divorce recovery group to help me in processing what was going on in my home before filing for divorce. In one of the movies we watched, they gave a literal formula for healing in terms of number of years in order to begin dating again. As helpful as the group was, I don't believe in a formula because we all have unique circumstances.

A person who was married for twenty years could be ready to be remarried after three years, whereas a person who has been married for three years could take ten years to recover. The various factors involved are length of time grieving, ability to grieve, obstacles to healing, complicated grief, ages of your children, situations around the divorce, as well as what happened several years leading up to the divorce.

What I will say is that if you can't seem to pull yourself together to get out the door, you are probably not ready. I would also say to be careful when it comes to feeling the pressure from your friends who have already decided to take the plunge into the dating arena.

There are several questions to ask yourself:

"Am I still bleeding out?"

"Am I placing God's will over my own?

"Why do I want to date?"

"Have I been alone with myself enough before I bring someone else into the picture?

"Am I looking for someone to complete me?"

Knowing who you are, what you're worth, and having the ability to set boundaries will also help you determine your readiness.

When we refuse to place our relationships (romantic, friendships, spouses, coworkers, ministry partners, etc.) on the altar, and give them to God, they become our idols. For some reason, as women, we equate being a woman to being married or with a man in general.

There are other things that we can do other than being with a man, i.e., serving others, worshipping God, teaching, evangelizing, and mentoring. When we are married, our desires are to our husbands, but in singlehood, they are to the Lord.

What did the apostle Paul tell us?

"For I would that all men were even as I myself. But every man hath his proper gift of God, one after this manner, and another after that.

I say therefore to the unmarried and widows, it is good for them if they abide even as I."

(1 Corinthians 7: 7-8, KJV)

Because you have already been through a divorce, and faced many other challenges, if nothing else is done, you want to make sure that you understand and break your unhealthy relationship patterns of behavior. When it comes to any problem, the best way to tackle it, is to get to the root of it. Staying on the surface, instead of pulling up that problem from the root, means you risk the problem resurfacing again.

Getting to the root of unhealthy relationship patterns means getting to the source, or origin of what started the coping mechanisms and dysfunctional behaviors.

When we think of cravings, we often think of food, and not relationships. Cravings are normal and the first part of the relationship cycle. As a matter of fact, they are nothing more than evidence that we are human. Sometimes we can get so holy that we think relationship cravings are wrong.

God created Eve so that she could satisfy Adam's craving for human relationships, even though he already had a relationship with God. God created us to crave relationship.

We get into trouble when our cravings lead to lust, or we place our craving for human relationship above our craving for relationship with God.

Our craving for relationship enables us to know that we were made for community.

"And the LORD God said, It is not good that the man should be alone; I will make him an help meet for him." (Genesis 2:18, KJV)

The second part of the relationship cycle is entering a relationship.

"And Isaac brought her into his mother Sarah's tent, and took Rebekah, and she became his wife; and he loved her: and Isaac was comforted after his mother's death." (Genesis 24:67, KJV)

When we enter a new relationship, it is like opening a door not knowing what's on the other side. One example would be watching some of the old game shows on TV. The contestant is told to pick a door. That door holds their prize.

Will you want to embrace what's inside, or take off running? Entering new relationships are the same way. Only time will tell what you have gotten yourself into.

It is normal for both parties to be overly concerned with putting on an impression for the other person. We want to be liked. And we want to appear to be agreeable. If one person says, "Let's go to the movies. What do you want to see?" Then, the other person may say, "Whatever you want to see."

Sometimes that is the case. We don't care about what it is. We just care about having companionship, doing the social thing, having the work-partnership.

Most times, we are people-pleasing, seeking to make that big impression, consumed with the other person liking us. No matter what kind of relationship it is, this plays out real fast. You get sick and tired of going along with everything someone else wants to do. The funny thing about this is that we are the ones who initiated it in the first place.

Now, we seek to come out of it. We want to make our voices known and heard. Be who we really are. Creating an empowered new chapter of life involves having emotional, mental, physical, and spiritual boundaries.

It is normal when a relationship first starts off to experience symbiosis, as we described above, where you are pretending to like everything that the other person likes. This slowly wears off and differentiation occurs. Differentiation is when the identity, or real self emerges. This real self has desires, needs, and its own wiring.

What differentiates a healthy relationship from a toxic relationship during the "Entering A Relationship Phase" is what happens in the beginning.

When you enter a toxic relationship, you are immediately "love-bombed." Love-bombed means you are swept off your feet and over-the-top lavished on. It feels too good to be true. You are given flowers, poetry, words of affirmation, opened doors, lots of teddy bears, gifts, candy, etc.

The spiritual energy emitted from the toxic individual is that of manipulation. You are literally intoxicated.

"The rulers of the Philistines went to her and said, "See if you can lure him into showing you the secret of his great strength and how we can overpower him so we may tie him up and subdue him. Each one of

us will give you eleven hundred shekels of silver."
(Judges 16:5, NIV)

Everybody knows about you. As a matter of fact, they seem to know more about you than you know about you.

Although this may seem natural, and nothing that should raise concern, it is. You just don't know that yet. But by the next part you will.

What seems to feel good; "this is my trophy, my woman, my display" show soon turns into you feeling like something is off. And not just a little bit. Something feels terribly off. An emotion starts creeping up that you are familiar with, but you can't place it.

That emotion is shame. You are bathing in it. Next thing you know, you are in the Garden of Eden, and covering yourself with leaves.

By the time our minds have caught up with what our bodies already know, we are then able to decide if something is a good thing or bad thing. Having all the attention on you may seem like a good thing. However, we must remember that the spiritual energy that accompanies being love-bombed is nothing good.

The energy is toxic. And it is the toxic spiritual energy that causes the reverse of what would be expected to happen.

The response itself is the warning sign. But again, if we are too caught up, we will miss it.

If we are not, it is then that we can stop, reassess the situation, and then use wisdom in whether to move forward.

Nine times out of ten, there is no stopping. No "Be still and know" moment.

You are intoxicated by being love-bombed. Knowing and feeling something is off but entangled in a web of energy that's indescribable.

"After putting him to sleep on her lap, she called for someone to shave off the seven braids of his hair, and so began to subdue him. And his strength left him."

(Judges 16:19, NIV)

The third phase of the toxic relationship cycle is the "unhealthy patterns of behavior/problems" occurring phase.

When unhealthy patterns of behavior occur in any relationship, some of the following may occur:

- Passive-aggressiveness
- Avoidance
- Anger

- Shutting down
- Walking Out
- Silent Treatment

In a toxic relationship, you have the additional part of flipping the script, guilt tripping, and playing games when you confront your partner about their behavior.

Codependency.

The first pattern of behavior that I want to talk about is codependency. Codependency in basic terms, is enabling. Codependents enable their spouses, partners, life-giving friends, family members, kids, coworkers, etc. to be irresponsible in whatever area that they are struggling in.

This enabling could be in the form of giving money for addictions, arguing back and forth with the person so that they make "their issue" your issue, or ignoring the behavior in general instead of creating boundaries for how we will live and or function going forward.

Once the honeymoon phase of a relationship is over, problems will occur. And to be honest, the problems started occurring before this phase was over. You were just so in love that you ignored them.

Just like dealing with a computer problem, you have to analyze the why in your relationship. Like all others sins, codependency is rooted in fear. Fear of the unknown.

- What will happen if you don't pay the bills?
- What will happen if you don't budget the money?

- What will happen if you don't iron his clothes?
- Will you end up homeless, broke, having to downsize?

The common areas of insecurities and or brokenness are low self-esteem, low self-worth, poor body image, and not enoughness. Codependents cover up these areas by becoming the Savior of the day in their spouse's, coworker's, friend's, or ministry partner's life.

So, even when you have the "come to Jesus moment" and stop doing things for the other person, if you don't take the time to do the self-work, you will be right back to wearing your cape as Savior of the day, and playing Jesus.

Frustration is the catalyst for change. However, that is only if the desire and hard work required to be a better version of you outweighs the pain of staying in the comfort zone of where you are now.

Think about a child tying their shoes. It is easier for us to do it for them than to hear them whining, "I can't do it!" But they don't learn that way.

It's the same thing for the codependent. Their spouse/partner/friend/coworker/ministry partner screams out and guess what? You run to the rescue instead of letting them struggle and figure it out. The only way to deal with a person who is irresponsible is to 1) Empathize, but not take over. "I know this must be hard for you." 2) Set strict boundaries. 3) Get help for yourself.

Arguing with an irresponsible person will have them to transfer their problem back over to you. You have to be able to ask yourself, "What happened in my childhood that made me think I had to solve everyone else's problems, even to the point of letting people disrespect me, walk over me like a doormat, and take all my money in the process?"

Addicted to Chaos.

Another unhealthy pattern of behavior is being addicted to chaos. Sometimes you don't want to change because you don't know what to do when you are not fighting in the relationship all the time.

Walking Out.

Or are you the one who does not want to deal with any of her issues, so every time your partner brings something up, you walk out the door, slam it, and leave?

Entanglement/Enmeshment.

When it comes to entanglement/enmeshment, things can get real tricky. Just like codependency.

Think about having ten necklaces tangled up together with several knots. This may sound farfetched. But it isn't. I have had it happen one too many times. It is not fun.

As a matter of fact, the more you try to untangle the mess, the more they get entangled. It is easier to get these necklaces tangled up than it is to untangle them. And before we know it, our emotions are entangled up with these necklaces.

The more that you try to untangle yourself from an entangled relationship, the more entangled you will become. Getting to the root of the entanglement is where healing begins. But it is also where the pain lies.

When you are entangled, you are literally being controlled by someone else's emotional state. Another way of looking at it is to picture your backyard and your neighbor's backyard. You both have fences. The fences serve as boundaries. However, you have decided to make your neighbor's yard free reign to go in and out as you please. You don't know where your fence ends and theirs begin.

"So Delilah said to Samson, "Please tell me where your great strength lies, and with what you may be bound to afflict you."

And Samson said to her, "If they bind me with seven fresh bowstrings, not yet dried, then I shall become weak, and be like any other man."

So the lords of the Philistines brought up to her seven fresh bowstrings, not yet dried, and she bound him with them. Now men were lying in wait, staying with her in the room.

And she said to him, "The Philistines are upon you, Samson!" But he broke the bowstrings as a strand *of yarn breaks when it touches fire. So the secret of his strength was not known.*

(Judges 16:6-9, NKJV)

Whenever you are in the third stage of the unhealthy relationship cycle, you start playing games with the other person in the toxic relationship. Samson and Delilah's game was called "Tell me the source." Samson gave her three answers before he gave in and told Delilah where his strength came from:

- Seven fresh bowstrings
- New ropes
- 7 braids sewn into the fabric on the loom and tightened with the pin.

Most women have played the "If you could just" game. In this game, you are given several things you need to do in order to get the relationship back to the beginning. Here is a list of the things that are usually said in the "If you could just game":

- Change your hair
- Dress differently
- Change your makeup
- Go back to school
- Wear different shoes

The fourth stage in the unhealthy relationship cycle is the languishing stage. In the languishing stage, you run after the other person in the toxic relationship. Not only are you running after them, you are working hard to come up with a plan to fix the other person.

As a matter of fact, you are burning the midnight oil. You know if you could just figure out the magic formula to fix this person, you would be on the right track. You might throw in a little manipulation need-be.

You have determined that you are all in, putting everything on the line to make the relationship work with this individual. Even if this means you are worn out in the process, it will be worth it. At least you will have your needs met.

The irony of the situation is that the harder you work, the more hopeless, confused, frustrated, defeated, and lonelier you become. You are literally in a state of languishing. If God has promised you a life of abundance, this couldn't be what it looks like.

Trying to fix/control the other person is going to bring resistance and immediate pushback. God created us out of love, and in that love, he gave us freedom.

Trying to fix/control that love means you are in turn setting up desires against that other person's will, which in turn, places them in bondage. Running after a person who is walking away from you emotionally, mentally, spiritually, and physically creates a toxic dance cycle.

That is why your efforts to lasso them back in is not working.

First, you have to address your root issues of control. Then, everything that needs to happen in order for you to be in a healthy relationship will fall in place.

If a person exits abruptly during your state of languishing, you still go through the same patterns of behavior trying to pull them back in. However, you are just living in two different locations trying to do it, i.e., the person has told you that it is over, and peaces out.

The next thing you know, you are popping up at events you know they will be attending just so you can see them and hope they will come to their senses. During this time, you end up disrespecting yourself even more, but unfortunately unable to see that.

The last stage in the Toxic Relationship Cycle is "The Exit." It is just what it says it is. Someone leaves. That someone is usually the man. And if he is allowed to come back, each time the abuse is more intense, and there is a shorter period time for the duration of the relationship.

"The Philistines grabbed him, gouged out his eyes, and took him down to Gaza. They shackled him in irons and put him to the work of grinding in the prison. But his hair, though cut off, began to grow again." (Judges 16:21-30, MSG)

Delilah peaced out on Samson. Yep. She got her money and left.

"When Delilah saw that he had told her everything, she sent word to the rulers of the Philistines, "Come back once more; he has told me

everything." So the rulers of the Philistines returned with the silver in their hands."

(Judges 16: 18-21, NIV)

She dropped the bomb on him and left. Just like Samson willingly gave away his power and identity when he hooked up with Samson and Delilah, we give away our power and identity when we get involved with toxic individuals.

Just in case you are not sure if the relationship you are currently in, or just came out of was toxic, and you need to review the behavior again before moving to the next chapter, here are the signs:

1. Love-bombed-intoxicating spiritual energy emitted, you are worshipped like a trophy, then dumped with shame.
2. Controls -where you go, who you see, who you talk to, what you say, how you say it.

3. Plays games-"if you could just"-change your hair, clothes, makeup, like a barbie doll.
4. Does things to purposely make you jealous, and then when it works, calls you insecure, jealous, and crazy.
5. Constantly judges and criticizes others-like a virus, you find yourself jumping on his bandwagon.
6. Isolates you from other people using various means---physically, emotionally, spiritually, mentally, and financially.
7. Your brokenness (unworthiness/not enoughness) is leading you in making decisions.
8. You are spiritually blinded, and you turn your head and ignore what is really going on.
9. You experience cognitive dissonance-what they are saying and doing and you are seeing is not lining up.

10. You are in bondage to the person-you have a soul tie, and you need them like a drug.

11. Everybody knows your business-as a matter of fact, they know more than you do about you.

12. Inconsistency-The person's words and actions are almost never matching up.

What Happens After You Leave?

You think that warfare existed while you were in the toxic relationship with the other person, spiritual warfare exists on a whole 'nother level when you leave.

One of the main ways that your ex will attack you is through a flat-out smear campaign. A smear campaign is just like a political campaign where you enlist people to vote for you. However, it is with the intent of destroying the other person completely because you are no longer with them.

It is also with the intent of the perpetrator making themselves look good. Smear campaigns are not just meant to destroy your character, they also exist to cheat you out of what rightfully belongs to you financially and property-wise.

Six things happen when you are dealing with the spirit of manipulation and entitlement during a smear campaign. And *1 Kings 21* spells it out perfectly.

1. The person feels entitled to get whatever they want because of proximity and title, even when it does not belong to them.
In verses 1-3, down below, we are told of how Ahab coveted Naboth's vineyard, which was close to his palace. Not only did he covet it, but he also felt entitled to it because he was king.

"And it came to pass after these things, that Naboth the Jezreelite had a vineyard, which was in Jezreel, hard by the palace of Ahab king of Samaria.

And Ahab spake unto Naboth, saying, Give me thy vineyard, that I may have it for a garden of herbs, because it is near unto my house: and I will give thee for it a better vineyard than it; or, if it seem good to thee, I will give thee the worth of it in money.

And Naboth said to Ahab, The LORD forbid it me, that I should give the inheritance of my father's unto thee." (1 Kings 21: 1-3, KJV)

You have found yourself in court with your ex, and the next thing you know, you are fighting to keep an inheritance that was given to you by your parents. And because the person was married to you, they feel entitled to take what rightfully belongs to you.

2. They sulk.

The next thing that happens is that they sulk a.k.a. pout like they are little children. Ahab was so outdone that someone would feel grounded, rooted, and worthy enough to stand up for themselves, and tell him, the King, "No!"

"And Ahab came into his house heavy and displeased because of the word which Naboth the Jezreelite had spoken to him: for he had said, I will not give thee the inheritance of my fathers. And he laid him down upon his bed, and turned away his face, and would eat no bread.

But Jezebel his wife came to him, and said unto him, Why is thy spirit so sad, that thou eatest no bread?

And he said unto her, Because I spake unto Naboth the Jezreelite, and said unto him, Give me thy vineyard for money; or else, if it please thee, I will give thee another vineyard for it: and he answered, I will not give thee my vineyard." (1 King 21:4-6, KJV)

You are in court trying to iron out all your financials and you find yourself in an unfortunate situation that presents itself like what went on with Ahab and Jezebel. The judges are not familiar with this person, and the next thing you know, they are wooed in through the spirit of manipulation, making the judge think that you are out to take all their money, and that somehow your inheritance belongs to him. This situation is more common than any of us would like to believe.

3. They falsify court documents.

"So she wrote letters in Ahab's name, and sealed them with his seal, and sent the letters unto the elders and to the nobles that were in his city, dwelling with Naboth.

And she wrote in the letters, saying, Proclaim a fast, and set Naboth on high among the people:

(1 Kings 21:8-9, KJV)

It is one thing for someone to lie on you. It is a whole 'nother level when someone lies on you in court and brings in falsified documents. But unfortunately, this is one of the default expectations when you are coming out of a toxic relationship.

You can expect income figures to be lowered and changed. Inheritances stolen. Any and everything under the sun is and has been done in the courtroom.

As you are going through the process, it becomes imperative to remind yourself and rest assured in the fact that God is the great "I AM". All we have to do is fill in the blank for whatever it is that we need him to be. In the case of a divorce process, although there are physical attorneys and judges present, we have to armor up, and look at God as being our representative in both areas.

Toxic relationship or not, living the Christian life is an all-out battle.

When I went through my divorce, somehow, I magically "had a PhD and tons of income coming in" according to my ex. I was appalled that the courts would believe it, given my kids and I were actually living in a state of poverty.

4. **They find accomplices who are willing to lie on their behalf.**

Jezebel, in her spirit of manipulation, or "take-over spirit", as church folk call it, enlisted two men to lie and accuse Naboth of blaspheming God. It does not get anymore scandalous than this.

"And set two men, sons of Belial, before him, to bear witness against him, saying, thou didst blaspheme God and the king. And then carry him out, and stone him, that he may die.

And the men of his city, even the elders and the nobles who were the inhabitants in his city, did as

Jezebel had sent unto them, and as it was written in the letters which she had sent unto them.

And there came in two men, children of Belial, and sat before him: and the men of Belial witnessed against him, even against Naboth, in the presence of the people, saying, Naboth did blaspheme God and the king. (1 Kings 21: 10-11, 13, KJV)

This is the definite scene of a TV courtroom show. The next thing you know, there are mutual friends of yours and your ex's, along with some of your family members and his in court lying and stating that the claims your ex-husband are making is true.

Somehow your inheritance belongs to him. And the more you try to explain yourself, the more the spirit of manipulation, deception, and entitlement is permeating.

5. They accomplish what they set out to do.

"And there came in two men, children of Belial, and sat before him: and the men of Belial witnessed against him, even against Naboth, in the presence of the people, saying, Naboth did blaspheme God and the king. Then they carried him forth out of the city, and stoned him with stones, that he died.

Then they sent to Jezebel, saying, Naboth is stoned, and is dead. (1 Kings 21: 10-14)

The judge believes your ex-husband. Not only has your inheritance been stolen, but you end up somehow owing your ex-husband money when the situation was the other way around when you first entered the courtroom.

At first, you think that you just didn't try hard enough. The "I AM NOT ENOUGH" banner starts wrapping around your body.

Then, you realize there are several things at play in your divorce proceedings: 1) lack of discernment by judges and attorneys, 2) an interest in the court system making money at all costs, 3) spiritual warfare to destroy you emotionally, mentally, spiritually, and physically, 4) a desire for the court system to side with the person who is making the most money, and in most cases, that is the man, and 5) Satan's plan for you to never reclaim your power and identity so you will know you are enough because of feeling defeated by the outcome.

The spirit of manipulation and narcissism in general has gotten ramped up to a whole 'nother level in our society, leaving us Christians with no other choice but to stay on our knees and fully armored on the battlefield. We don't have time to slack up now. We have work to do.

We are fighting against Satan in the boxing ring. His job is to knock us out, so he can knock out our children, their children, and so on. He wants us to operate from an armor of generational curses instead of the armor of God. We cannot let that happen.

6. God judges.

And it came to pass, when Jezebel heard that Naboth was stoned, and was dead, that Jezebel said to Ahab, Arise, take possession of the vineyard of Naboth the Jezreelite, which he refused to give thee for money: for Naboth is not alive, but dead.

And it came to pass, when Ahab heard that Naboth was dead, that Ahab rose up to go down to the vineyard of Naboth the Jezreelite, to take possession of it.

And the word of the LORD came to Elijah the Tishbite, saying,

Arise, go down to meet Ahab king of Israel, which is in Samaria: behold, he is in the vineyard of Naboth, whither he is gone down to possess it.

And thou shalt speak unto him, saying, Thus saith the LORD, Hast thou killed, and also taken possession? And thou shalt speak unto him, saying, Thus saith the LORD, In the place where dogs licked the blood of Naboth shall dogs lick thy blood, even thine.

And Ahab said to Elijah, Hast thou found me, O mine enemy? And he answered, I have found thee: because thou hast sold thyself to work evil in the sight of the LORD.

Behold, I will bring evil upon thee, and will take away thy posterity, and will cut off from Ahab him that pisseth against the wall, and him that is shut up and left in Israel,

And will make thine house like the house of Jeroboam the son of Nebat, and like the house of Baasha the son of Ahijah, for the provocation wherewith thou hast provoked me to anger, and made Israel to sin.

*And of Jezebel also spake the L*ORD*, saying, The dogs shall eat Jezebel by the wall of Jezreel.*

Him that dieth of Ahab in the city the dogs shall eat; and him that dieth in the field shall the fowls of the air eat.

*But there was none like unto Ahab, which did sell himself to work wickedness in the sight of the L*ORD*, whom Jezebel his wife stirred up.*

*And he did very abominably in following idols, according to all things as did the Amorites, whom the L*ORD *cast out before the children of Israel.*

And it came to pass, when Ahab heard those words, that he rent his clothes, and put sackcloth upon his flesh, and fasted, and lay in sackcloth, and went softly.

And the word of the LORD came to Elijah the Tishbite, saying,

Seest thou how Ahab humbleth himself before me? because he humbleth himself before me, I will not bring the evil in his days: but in his son's days will I bring the evil upon his house.

(1 Kings 21:13-29, KJV)

Sometimes your ex-husband has to suffer the consequences of his actions immediately. Sometimes he has to answer to God in heaven. Whatever the case, it is your job to keep yourself on the right path to healing and reclaiming your power and identity, and not get caught up in the consequences that are faced.

If you are not careful, you can allow a smear campaign to destroy you. Why? It deflects from the real issues at hand, i.e., healing, you and your children's emotional, mental, physical, and spiritual well-being, visitation schedules, the division of assets, and more importantly, getting the divorce and post issues done.

The other thing that happens is that Satan will try to work so much on your heart with bitterness, resentment, and unforgiveness, that you can easily end up with those same spirits lying inside of your heart and soul because of what you feel is justice is not what God feels is justice.

God is a constant. His character and faithfulness remain the same. Never-changing. Always forgiving and willing to give us another chance.

Like Jonah, the temptation can be to get so caught up in worrying about how God is going to give justice to your ex, that you allow yourself to sit under a tree, hot and irritated, in a state of bitterness and resentment.

Anger is part of the process. It should not be stifled or ignored. However, you still have work to do. And your work is in reclaiming your power and identity, and healing yourself, and allow God to focus on being God.

Remember, to reclaim your power and identity after being in a toxic relationship is to move forward with your life by healing, taking responsibility for your part, forgiving your ex and yourself, and doing the work to become the best version of yourself possible.

Build Resilience and Flourish

Healing is an emotional, mental, spiritual, and physical process. And each of these processes use energy. Resilience is the art form of being able to bounce back after having emotional, mental, physical, and spiritual traumas, stresses, and tribulations.

Respecting our process with self-care is part of building resilience and flourishing. Not respecting our process will lead to burnout, and an inability to flourish in any manner. Flourishing is another word for thriving.

When you are thriving, you are in environments that foster and nurture autonomy, growth, respect, and a desire to lead, and not just manage. Anybody can manage a group of people. Not anybody can lead them. Leading involves having a certain amount of emotional intelligence and servanthood. In essence, you are bringing out the best in your people, not yourself.

God designed rest in mind with the thought that we would operate from its place, not its force. Either we respect rest, and operate in life from its place, or we disrespect it, and operate in life from being a slave to it.

Those words might sound crazy, but they are not. When we respect rest, we have control over when it happens. When we disrespect rest, we are out of control, and we are slaves to the process. In other words, we are forced down even when we don't want to be down because we turned a blind ear to what our minds, body, and souls were telling us all along.

Healing is serious business. But so is rest. Resting relieves us of the slavery mentality. Therefore, God created Sabbath. He rested on the seventh day. He did not need to. However, everything that God does is in mind with being first an example of what he teaches and preaches.

There are two things that happen when rest is ignored. The first one is that it allows the spirit of manipulation to get a foothold and target us. The second thing is that it creates obstacles for building resilience and flourishing.

There are five signs that the lack of self-care is enabling the spirit of manipulation to target you:

Sign Number 1: You take off running.

You are in the process of trying to get your life back together. You get a message from your ex: "I'm taking the kids and you will never see them again. And not only that, but I'm also telling everyone what you did."

This is nothing different from what has been said before. Only this time, you have not been practicing self-care. No self-care=bad judgment calls.

You flee your house with your kids, luggage, and all headed to a hotel or who knows where. Your nervous system is jacked up because of all the things that you have already been through, and so, the lack of self-care has actually added to it.

Later on, you guys return home, and you have a "come to Jesus" moment on how things could have played out differently if you had had enough rest.

This may sound like some fictitious situation. But it isn't. Unfortunately, this was me several years ago, fleeing like the devil himself had gotten hold of me.

Elijah took off running in 1 Kings 19:2-3, *"Then Jezebel sent a messenger unto Elijah saying, "So let the gods to me, and more also, if I make not thy life of one of them by tomorrow about this time.*

And when he saw that, he arose and went for his life, and came to Beersheeba, which belongeth to Judah, and left his servants there.

Sign Number 2: You don't enlist help.

Elijah left his servant there. So, if Jezebel was truly after him, what was he going to do by himself? And if someone was truly after you, would you have been able to make the judgment call, and enlist the police and/or friends for help? Everything is handled differently when you are not operating from a place of rest.

Sign Number 3: You lose your identity.

Once Elijah got to the cave, God asked him, "What doest thou here, Elijah?"

God really did not want to ask him what he was doing there. The deeper question was, "Who are you, cause I seriously think you have forgotten?"

Elijah was God's son, a prophet, slayer of 450 false prophets of Baal, fervent prayer when it came to rain, recipient of food by ravens and brooks, witness to miracles of fire from heaven, and he was running from Jezebel? Makes no sense at all. But if you look back, it made perfect sense.

NO self-care + no help=burnout + bad judgment.

After leaving your toxic relationship, God is asking you the same question he asked me when I fled from my home, "What are you doing here, running from a threat you have heard repeatedly, knowing that it is with the intent of getting a rise out of you?"

Sign Number 4: The spirit of depression comes.

"But he himself went a day's journey into the wilderness, and came and sat down under a juniper tree: and he requested for himself that he might die; and said, It is enough; now, O Lord, take away my life; for I am not better than my fathers." (1 Kings 19:4, KJV)

It got really dramatic, but Elijah was feeling hopeless.

And you are saying, "I want out of here! I can't take him anymore!" And without practicing self-care after leaving a toxic relationship, you will feel like that and even more. Lack of self-care means you can't build resilience emotionally, mentally, spiritually, or physically.

No resilience=no flourishing.

When you are taking care of everyone else and not making yourself a priority, your kids cannot thrive. And it is because you are not thriving.

Sign Number 5: Pride comes in through the spirit of self-pity.

Notice the word "self" is there. It means you take pride in victimhood. Then, you yourself become toxic. Self-pity repels people.

"And he said, "I have been very jealous for the Lord God of hosts: for the children of Israel have forsaken thy covenant, thrown down thine altars, and slain thy prophets with the sword; and I, even I only; am left; and they seek my life, to take it away." (1 Kings 19:10, KJV)

One person told Elijah that they would kill him. That one person was Jezebel. Somehow, "she" turned into a "they".

Pride in the form of self-pity always brings skewed thinking.

Other people talk to you, and they hear you saying things like:

"I'm the only one dealing with a toxic relationship."

"You have one child and I have six."

"Well, at least you have help, I'm out here all alone."

"I'm recovering from this relationship and still having to do ministry."

The list of extreme comparative suffering quotes goes on and on. Guess what though?

Just like a "be still and know" moment happened for Elijah under that tree AFTER he rested, we have that same assurance. He rested, slept, and ate, then rested, slept, and ate again. Then, he heard God's voice in the cave.

God gave him explicit instructions:

"And the LORD said unto him, Go, return on thy way to the wilderness of Damascus: and when thou comest, anoint Hazael to be king over Syria:

And Jehu the son of Nimshi shalt thou anoint to be king over Israel: and Elisha the son of Shaphat of Abelmeholah shalt thou anoint to be prophet in thy room.

And it shall come to pass, that him that escapeth the sword of Hazael shall Jehu slay: and him that escapeth from the sword of Jehu shall Elisha slay.

Yet I have left me seven thousand in Israel, all the knees which have not bowed unto Baal, and every mouth which hath not kissed him." (1 Kings 19:15-18, KJV)

In other words, God told him, "You ain't the only one left." Those in toxic relationships: "You are dealing with a lot. And it feels like way too much for one person. And it is when we are doing it without

God's help and a few other people in our corner. However, you are not th only one dealing with problems.

The devil has skewed your vision.

Remember: You are already enough. And you can build resilience and flourish. Start reclaiming your power and identity today.

Now, we are going to talk about the five ways that you create obstacles for yourself in building resilience and flourishing.

Number 1: You need to be needed.

You create a seat for yourself based on rejection. Somebody rejected you and it led you to feel the need to perform to be accepted. Moses liked being the judge. Performing this job made him feel accepted.

"And it came pass on the morrow, that Moses sat to judge the people: and the people stood by Moses from the morning unto the evening." (Exodus 18:13, KJV)

How do we know that Moses felt rejected? Take a look at verse number three in the same chapter to see evidence of Moses' engrained rejection from his family, the Egyptians, and then his wife's family: *"And her two sons: of which the name of the one was Gershom; for he said, I have been an alien in a strange land."*

Number 2: You don't create boundaries around the people you are helping.

You allow people twenty-four-hour access to you via email, phone and DM's. If it is a toxic relationship, all night and day access mean emotionally, mentally, spiritually, and physically drained after engagement.

And unlike dealing with other people, toxic individuals say that they want your advice, but they really don't.

Their main goal is to hog your time, expecting you to stop everything you are doing to hear them out. But, when their kids, husband, family, or whoever calls or comes in the door, their response is basically, "See ya, wouldn't want to be ya!" They won't reciprocate.

Number 3: You think the only way for people to have a "Come to Jesus" moment is through you.

God can use anyone or anything to get people's attention. He used a donkey to get Balaam's. Sometimes we have to let someone else be the person who gets the message across to that person who is hurting.

What was Moses' response when his father-in-law basically asked him, "What are you doing?"

"And Moses said unto his father-in-law, because the people come unto me to enquire of God:" (Exodus 18:15, KJV)

Although Moses was not toxic, when it comes to toxic people, they use "seeking God's will" as a coverup for their brokenness. Their actions almost never line up to their words. Their actions also show they want to remain the same because they refuse to be accountable and teachable.

Number 4: Someone has to come along and correct you.

"And Moses' father-in-law said unto him, the thing that thou doest is not good." (Exodus 18:17, KJV)

Other people have to open our eyes to our codependent behaviors by saying things like the following:

"You keep jumping in to save the day."

"I see that this person is weighing you down."

How we respond to this correction determines how we move ahead.

Number 5: You begin suffering from the symptoms of burnout.

You are emotionally, spiritually, and physically exhausted. What led up to this? Running everything and taking care of everyone by yourself. Why? You need to be needed and you have not gotten down to the root cause of why.

We can't inhale physical toxins and think we will be okay physically. We end up with toxic poisoning and cancer in our bodies. Since our mind, body, and soul are connected, when we hang out with toxic people on a regular basis, we receive the toxins that they are pouring out from their emotional and mental issues, affecting us not only physically, but mentally, emotionally, and spiritually.

At this point, you can't even help yourself, let alone anybody else. We can only help others when we have poured into ourselves. And not just poured into us but pouring into ourselves to the point of us having an overflow. It's kind of like pouring tea into a teacup, and then overflowing the cup to the point of the tea going into the saucer. People need to receive our overflow.

The first thing to remedy this situation is to:

1) **Become self-aware of your emotional threshold.**

Take the "be still and know moment" where you gain quiet time, clarity, and stillness – a break from the

Energizer bunny that keeps going and going. During this time, you are going to do several things:

   a. Ask yourself what message your mind, body, and soul are telling you. (Are they locking up, stiffening, tensing, holding your emotions, screaming out inside?)
   b. Ask yourself what you are going to do with this information.
   c. Write down the informational memories that are attached to your thoughts, making you behave the way that you have been behaving.
   d. Write down a plan to tackle your revelations.
   e. Write down a micro-plan where you break down this plan into manageable pieces.
   f. Celebrate making steps to move forward.

2) **Knowing and respecting our emotional threshold is the key to building resilience and flourishing.**

There are so many situations that we encounter in life that carry heavy emotional weight. Death and divorce are two of them. They require major self-care. Everything else needs to take a backseat.

When we keep going, and taking on other people's problems, and pretending like things are status quo, we eventually crash. The crashing occurs because we disrespected our emotional threshold. Death and divorce come with a compromised immune system, along with a ball of emotions going on at all times.

Job loss and financial devastation carries heavy emotional weight. We have to take time to deal with the loss. You also can't tell everybody and their momma what is going on.

Your question is probably, "Why?" Everybody and their momma have their opinion of what happened, how it happened, why it happened, what you should do, and what you shouldn't do. Just that alone causes overwhelm. And you are already overwhelmed.

A lot of it is sincere. However, we as Christians can make people feel worse. We spiritually bypass with scriptures when we don't want to experience other people's emotions or want them to get back to their "old self".

Another thing we do is to invoke other people with self-doubt and fear. The last thing that a person needs when they are following what God has told them, is for someone else to say, "Ok. I understand God told you that. But, how are you going to make it?" If this person has heard from God, we need to respect it. And follow that respect with prayer.

The person who is going through does not need the fear and self-doubt when all they have is their faith to hold on to. They are using all their resources possible to maintain that "peace that surpasses all understanding".

The very last thing they need is someone telling them ten things that will happen to them as a result of them being in that situation. Nine times out of ten, they already know that. They don't need an alarm clock. They don't need the "would have", "should have", "could have", "never", and "always" -false keywords statements.

They need friends sitting with them, praying for and with them, and hoping and praying for the best. And as the old folks used to say back in the day, "If you can't say nothing good, say nothing at all." Remember the story of Jesus healing the girl? He had to send the unbelievers outside so that his faith would be contained inside, and the girl could arise:

> *"Get out!" he told them. "The girl isn't dead; she's only asleep." But the crowd laughed at him. After the crowd was put outside, however, Jesus went in and took the girl by the hand, and she stood up!"*
> *(Matthew 9: 23-25, NLT)*

3) Know when to accept advice from emotionally, mentally, physically, and spiritually wise people.

Moses accepted advice from his father-in-law. Here is the actual recording of this interaction:

> *"Listen now to me and I will give you some advice, and may God be with you. You must be the people's representative before God and bring their disputes to him. Teach them his decrees and instructions, and show them the way they are to live and how they are to behave.*
>
> *But select capable men from all the people—men who fear God, trustworthy men who hate dishonest gain—*

and appoint them as officials over thousands, hundreds, fifties and tens.

Have them serve as judges for the people at all times, but have them bring every difficult case to you; the simple cases they can decide themselves. That will make your load lighter, because they will share it with you. If you do this and God so commands, you will be able to stand the strain, and all these people will go home satisfied."

Moses listened to his father-in-law and did everything he said. He chose capable men from all Israel and made them leaders of the people, officials over thousands, hundreds, fifties and tens. They served as judges for the people at all times. The difficult cases they brought to Moses, but the simple ones they decided themselves.

(Exodus 18: 19-26, NIV)

Take a "be still and know" moment and decide who you will take advice from.

Healing After Job, Church, and Family Hurt

Whether it's job, church, or family hurt, you were hurt by groups of people who run on systems. They can be categorized under a conflict-resolution system, a passive-aggressive system, or a blame-game system.

Conflict- resolution systems are not void of problems. They have problems and handle these problems according to scripture. Solutions to their problems are handled with the involved parties, and oftentimes, the leadership as well.

This is also not saying that people won't have their feelings hurt in the process. They will. Conflict – resolution does not mean pain-free. Conflict resolution means you are handling conflict, not ignoring the problems, nor blaming someone else.

> *"If your brother sins against you, go and tell him his fault, between you and him alone. If he listens to you, you have gained your brother. But if he does not listen, take one or two others along with you, that every charge may be established by the evidence of two or three witnesses. If he refuses to listen to them, tell it to the church. And if he refuses to listen even to the church, let him be to you as a Gentile and a tax collector."*
>
> *(Matthew 18:15-17, ESV)*

When it comes to the blame-game system, it is a whole 'nother story. Every member in either of these three locations (job, church, family) are picking one person to be the scapegoat. Literally everything that is going on in the world is this person's fault.

How in the world could this be? It is not the truth. But it is how this system functions and will continue to function for years.

This system consists of one to three problem people. Everybody knows who they are. But they are not dealing with it. Their way of dealing with it is pacifying the problem individuals whose behavior is either "Everything is all about me", or "I only want to use you."

Not only are they not dealing with it, but they are also adding to the problem. How is that? They sit and listen to the malicious lies, judging, and criticizing from these problem people, and will not say a mumbling word. Even when they know that the person is lying and has a lack of integrity overall.

Either someone in this system gets tired and pulls out of it, and the situation comes to a head, or it literally continues happening in that family, job, or church until Jesus comes.

The excuse for the people who are not saying anything is that they are keeping peace. As my therapist asked me before, "At what expense?"

The other problem is that the person who has been drafted as the scapegoat is usually more of the reserved type, walking around with the "I AM NOT ENOUGH / UNWORTHINESS" banner on, and is also needing to speak up in order to gain respect.

This is where I used to fit in perfectly. People knew that I wasn't going to say anything, and thus, they acted accordingly, doing anything and everything to walk all over me. I was more concerned with people-pleasing to avoid rejection than respecting myself.

How do you know that you are walking around with a spirit of unworthiness? I'm glad that you asked. There are seven signs.

Sign Number 1: You are the scapegoat | poison container | punching bag for any and all of your family.

With Abraham's family, the sin of deception was running rampant. Abraham lied about Sarah. He said she was his sister. Isaac lied about Rebekah. He said she was his sister. Lying. Wives. Sisters. Hmmm. Soap opera drama, right?

Jacob (known as the trickster) stole Esau's birthright. Rebekah and Jacob stole Esau's blessing by gluing on animal fur. Isaac thought something was a little shady when it came to Jacob's voice but went on and blessed him anyway.

The soap opera gets better. Jacob goes to Padan-Aram to escape being murdered after stealing the blessing. He falls in love with Rachel, his Uncle Laban' daughter, expects to marry her, but then good ol' Uncle Laban with the help of Leah tricks him into marrying Leah instead.

I hope you're holding on to your seat at this point.

I guess Jacob had too much to drink since he didn't know who he was marrying till morning came. Here's the catcher: Leah felt so unworthy that she married Jacob, knowing full well he was in love with her sister.

And unfortunately, the spirit of deception continued with Joseph and his brothers.

With you, everything under the sun goes on in your family, and you are blamed for it. And not only are you blamed for it, but you are also handled like a child without any needs, thoughts, or convictions of your own.

One person is mad. Ok! Dump it all on her.

Their kids are going through, you know. Ok! Dump it all on her. He doesn't want to take responsibility for the mess he created. Ok! Dump it all on her.

Being a willing participant of someone sinning against you is not keeping the peace. Sometimes silence is needed. Other times silence equals agreement and enabling sin.

The reason they keep doing what they are doing is because they know that you are not going to say anything. The moment you do, the tables are turned.

Brokenness attracts brokenness.

Change attracts change.

When we know our worth, we don't sign up to participate in foolishness. When we don't know our worth, we say to ourselves, *"I deserve to be talked to like this. I deserve for my soul to absorb death words."*

Sign Number 2: Your man is going to fill the void of your unworthiness.

Because we are all broken, we will always give people what we have from a broken lens. We will only reach perfection in heaven. Until then, other people cannot and will not fit the bill.

We were designed to only be fulfilled and content by the worthiness that is obtained through our relationship with God, and God alone.

You keep trying to have your man make you feel good about being you. And it is not just your man. It is your boss, your coworkers, friends, people at church, etc.

And so did Leah when she became a baby-making factory: *"Surely the Lord hath looked upon my affliction; now therefore my husband will love me. (Genesis 29:32, KJV)*

Somehow she didn't read that newspaper column that said, "He doesn't want you, Baby!"

Sign Number 3: Your baby is going to make the man fill your void.

This is the oldest lie in the book that Satan has led us women to believe. We can have 50 babies. Only having a "come to Jesus" moment about already having what you have been searching for through Christ's redemption on the cross, and our birthright being given to us because of God's adoption, and healing from the source of what or who made you unworthy/not good enough is going to fix the problem.

Having kids only exacerbates our already underlying issues of brokenness on both sides.

Whatever didn't get worked out before will be magnified and come to the light.

"And she conceived again, and bare a son; and said, Now this time will my husband be joined unto me, because I have born him three sons: therefore was his name called Levi."

(Genesis 29:34, KJV)

Sign Number 4: The spirit of unworthiness bleeds out everywhere.

It's on your kids, your extended family. Everywhere. No matter what you say or do, or where you go, your posture and behavior bleed out, "I'm not enough."

"And when Rachel saw that she bare Jacob no children, Rachel envied her sister; and said unto Jacob, Give me children or else I die. "

(Genesis 30:1, KJV)

Once this little fiasco didn't work, Rachel resorted to giving her husband to her handmaid. Talk about Leah's bleeding out!

Sign Number 5: The spirit of unworthiness brings on a spirit of competition, deception, lying, envy, etc.

As we can see, Abraham's family already has the spirit of deception under their belt. But now, they have been introduced to a few more.

"And Rachel said, with great wrestlings have I wrestled with my sister, and I have prevailed: and she called his name Napthali."

(Genesis 30:8, KJV)

Leah felt the need to keep up with her sister and her handmaid. So, she in turn gave her handmaid to Jacob. Then, she had two more sons.

What happens is that Satan gets into the minds of our family members, coworkers, ministry partners, friends, etc., making them go to Fantasy Island to conjure up a competition with us that never existed.

They say things like:

"I will buy more Farmhouse décor, the latest SUV, design a mansion, and go into debt in order to keep up with her."

"Oh, she gained weight. Now, I can compete with her. I have won the battle."

What battle?

At one of the companies I worked for, there was some weird behavior going on with the employees. It was triggering, and initially, I couldn't figure out for the life of me its catalyst, or what was driving it. I had already worked in a completely toxic environment at a manufacturing company, and I did not want to repeat it.

Finally, it did not take long to come up with the source. There was a certain quota that had to be filled to work in that particular role. People took it so seriously that they based their worthiness on that number because that's where their praise came from.

However, this setup a spirit of competition among the coworkers where they began stealing their fellow coworkers' numbers and lying and reporting the numbers as their own. Next thing you know, the spirit of envy, anger, control, etc. was added on in the environment. The whole environment became sick and toxic.

Just like the situation between Rachel and Leah, this was all over numbers. This is what happens with the spirit of unworthiness. You allow petty things to become major things. Or in the case of not speaking up for yourself after being used, you allow major things to manifest themselves as minor things.

Sign Number 6: Your children have adopted your false beliefs/superstitions about resolving your unworthiness.

Kids need something physical/tangible to rationalize things, or they use themselves. Their motto becomes:

"It's me. I'm the problem. I will be perfect, and then my mom and dad won't have a problem."

In Leah's case, her son is hunting for mandrakes- mandrakes were the superstition of bringing fertility and having a love potion attached to them.

"And Reuben went in the days of wheat harvest, and found mandrakes in the field, and brought them unto his

mother Leah. Then Rachel said to Leah, Give me, I pray thee, of thy son's mandrakes."

(Genesis 30:14, KJV)

Sign Number 7: You lower your standards in your romantic relationship and every other relationship.

She traded mandrakes for time with her husband. You settle for a piece of a man instead of one that respects you. A piece of a man is like a pit stop relationship (a five-dollar fill-up), that leaves you running on empty. You will find yourself questioning whether you are a Christian because you have lowered your standards believing that if you participate in this or that, it will solve the problem. It doesn't.

It brings on shame and more unworthiness. And shame begets shame. The next thing you know, you are asking yourself, "How did I get here?"

Wanting your worthiness to be filled by that man instead of God is how you got there. Refusing to dig deeper to get to the source of the problem is how you got there.

You are already enough. You can reclaim your power and identity. Your worthiness and enoughness is only found in Christ.

Lastly, I will dissect the passive-aggressive system. In this system there are problems going on that have been ignored for a long time. The spirit of avoidance, anger, bitterness, and resentment is present.

Why?

No one is dealing with the big elephant in the room. In this system, people alternate between walking around in a hostile state, and a passive-aggressive state, without doing anything about it.

After the roles of the people in charge get switched around, some big, dramatic incident occurs to get everybody to pay attention to the big elephant in the room. But guess what? They pay attention to it, but they don't do anything.

After the big blowup occurs, people go right back to doing what they were doing: ignoring the problem. It is unbelievable! No one has had a "come to Jesus" moment because they did not take a "be still and know" moment.

So, what can you do if you are trying to process hurt from being in the blame game or passive aggressive system currently or in the past?

First, take a "be still and know moment". *That is always number one.* And remember, that length of time will be different for everyone.

Then, you admit the truth. Not the Fantasy Island version. You admit the truth by writing out the answers to these questions:

- *Who hurt me?*
- *What did they do?*
- *When did they do it?*
- *Where did they do it?*
- *How did they do it?*
- *Why did they do it?*

The next thing that you need to do is to allow yourself to feel the grief because it's a comin'.

After allowing yourself to grieve, then remind yourself that you can only control you.

You cannot rewrite or revise history.

There is no would have, should have, could have because it's over.

Write down what part you played in the situation.

Give yourself time for more "be still and know moments" and grieving.

Resist self-blame and shaming. Forgive yourself and the person who sinned against you.

Decide whether or not you need to reconcile, restore, or leave the relationship with no closure.

If you decide to stay in the relationship, decide on what boundaries you are going to set. Otherwise, you will be on a wash, rinse, fold and repeat cycle.

Sometimes the worst thing that we can do is to continuously place commas in a relationship, and God has already placed periods.

After all of that, ask yourself how you will move forward. What will be the new chapter you are writing?

Then, move forward. Like David. He had a "come to Jesus" moment and realized that continuously mourning over a situation that had died would have killed him in the process.

Obstacles to Healing

When we sign up to do the hard work of healing, we have to armor up. Healing is not for the faint of heart. And it is not something that we can do in our own strength.

"Put on the whole armour of God, that ye may be able to stand against the wiles of the devil.

For we wrestle not against flesh and blood, but against principalities, against powers, against the rulers of the darkness of this world, against spiritual wickedness in high places.

Wherefore take unto you the whole armour of God, that ye may be able to withstand in the evil day, and having done all, to stand.

Stand therefore, having your loins girt about with truth, and having on the breastplate of righteousness;

And your feet shod with the preparation of the gospel of peace;

Above all, taking the shield of faith, wherewith ye shall be able to quench all the fiery darts of the wicked.

And take the helmet of salvation, and the sword of the Spirit, which is the word of God:

Praying always with all prayer and supplication in the Spirit, and watching thereunto with all perseverance and supplication for all saints;"

(Ephesians 6:11-18, KJV)

When we are under construction, we will battle all kinds of demonic forces.

The bottom line is that Satan does not want us to live victoriously and abundantly. And he will place anything and everything in our path to prevent that from happening.

Culture.

Believe it or not, one of the main obstacles of healing can be our very own families. And this includes both immediate and extended. Culture plays a major role in that it molds us into thinking that this is what we have to do because we are this or that nationality, ethnicity, or race.

Family culture plays a major role in how we operate in the world. Some families believe that no one, not even the children, should walk around crying, because it is a weakness.

In these kinds of settings, when a child is hurt, their parents' automatic reactions are usually, "You're fine! Stop crying!" Whether good or bad, the child is crying for a reason. But what happens is that living up to culture can tend to outweigh their needs.

I am a black woman. And when it comes to black women, we have the strong black woman, angry black woman, and black superwoman stereotypes in our culture.

The strong black woman stereotype means that we can have anything to happen to us, but we just keep on going. Black women are resilient. They are not invincible. Holding on to this stereotype will prevent us from healing like we need to because we associate being strong with not crying or showing emotion period.

The angry black woman stereotype is almost a gaslighting stereotype in a sense. Whenever black women get upset about something, other people can feel entitled to walk around and point fingers at us and say, "This is an angry black woman." In other words, "You have no right to get angry. Nothing happened."

God created all of us in his image. This image includes black woman. And he created all of us with emotions that need to be expressed when injustice occurs. We do not have to feel compelled to be depressed (anger turned inward) because parts of society want to keep us with a slavery mindset.

During slavery times, when the families were on the auctioning block, the men were forced to not show any emotion at all, as anything, and everything was done to their women and children. Exhibiting any kind of disagreement with what was taking place could cause them their lives. And thus, blacks learned to suppress their anger, and emotions in general. Then, you have the other sad side where men were forced to dance and perform and smile so that the possible buyers could decide if they wanted them. Forced emotions under devastating circumstances.

In society now, there is still a struggle for us to release our emotions because of what happened over four hundred years ago. Finding a balance in knowing whether it is safe to display our emotions or hide them has continued to be our struggle.

One fear that black women have, and blacks in general, is that once they start crying, they will become overwhelmed, and never be able to stop. I suffered from this problem for a good, long time. No matter how much my therapist and friends told me that I would bottom out, for some reason, I thought that it was not possible for me.

The more I became familiar with my emotions, the more I realized that yes, there is a bottom to crying. Even after crying for several hours, there is a bottom.

Lastly, the black superwoman is the stereotype that exists to say that black women can do it all without being affected. According to whom? Like I always say when I get the opportunity to speak to women in general: "We are not Energizer bunnies. We can't keep going and going."

With our superwoman capes on, we try to handle all the emotional, mental, spiritual, and physical needs of every family member on our own. We have to enlist help and know our limits. What society doesn't tell you is that burnout is rearing its ugly head right around the corner.

Other families' cultures may be that you hide everything from everyone. If something happens, just sweep it under the rug. But how long can you keep sweeping until the problem under the rug comes out?

In some families, any kind of vulnerability is seen as a sin, and so if something is wrong with you,

you have to walk around pretending like everything is fine, or like people are mind readers and should already know what is going on. One family member may cry out, "No one came to see me in the hospital." And then another member's reply is usually, "No one even knew you were sick."

Suppressed emotions can only go on for so long before a person either explodes or ends up with some other type of emotional or mental disorder. We were not created to function this way. What we can't express gets sent to our bodies and souls as another form of toxicity.

There are still other family cultures in which the men believe that women are uneducated, unworthy, and unknowledgeable, and unable to make decisions in general. If you already believe that your life carries no worth, why would you seek out a therapist for help?

Grief

Another obstacle to healing is grief. We touched on it a little bit in the previous section on culture. However, in this section, we will explore it a little bit more.

Grief can be an obstacle to healing in that if you are not sure what it entails, you could easily react by stuffing it. When I say stuffing it, I am referring to feeling like you are going to cry heavily, and then purposely preventing it from happening. In the beginning of my healing journey after divorce and compounded trauma, I was so afraid of the grief taking over, that I stuffed it, literally to the point of feeling sick.

It came to a head, and I will spare you the gross details. I will say this: About four meals in a row did not make it down for digestion.

Trust me, I never recommend anyone doing this. I had to learn the hard way unfortunately. It took me a while to learn that if it is a bad wave, then I need to excuse myself, and go to the bathroom, and let it out. Nothing is that important where we allow ourselves to get caught up and then pay for it later.

Because of the necessity to be released, prolonged stuffing often makes you prone for a public meltdown when it could have possibly been avoided.

One thing about grief is that it doesn't announce itself by going, "Hey, I'm getting ready to invade your space for a few minutes." No. It comes, and when it comes, the best thing to do is to hold on to Jesus as your anchor to help you to ride its waves.

There are no two people who have the same grief cycle. Some of my friends who have gone through similar drama as myself grieved for three hours a day for two to three years. My grief was more like off and on all day for two to three months straight, with a month break, and then back up again.

There is no correct frequency. The important thing to remember is that you allow it to happen. Not doing so will leave you feeling even more out of control than when it sneaks up on you. Why? Like a plumbing pipe, that is backed up and then unstopped, there is not going to be a pretty display when its contents are expelled, i.e., my moment above.

What became both a blessing, and an eye opener after reading an article on trauma, was the realization that trauma and grief cannot occur simultaneously. This brought on an extreme sense of relief. And if you have experienced trauma, I know that you know full well what it is that I am talking about.

Any sense of relief is welcomed. Imagine having a bad case of indigestion, and you start thinking to yourself, I should probably go and get some ginger ale. But then, you think to yourself, "Naaah, I'll just keep working on this paper until I get it done. I have to meet this deadline. It can wait."

Two hours later you feel miserable. Absolutely miserable. No amount of ginger ale or antacids does the trick. You feel like you are literally dying, or about to have a heart attack, one. This is what happens when we have several rounds of suppressing the grief and emotions that are trapped in our bodies. It forms a bottleneck, making you feel so miserable, you wish you had stopped typing that paper, having that telephone conversation, or doing whatever it was that you were doing, that you felt was more important at the time.

I have done it several times. One of two things always happens if I do it: 1) the grief gets stuck somewhere in my body, and I feel miserable or 2) the grief translates over to trauma, and it triggers down into crying on the floor TMJ pain, and I think I'm dying.

On one occasion during Covid-19, I was at work enrolling Chromebooks. I started to encounter some bad grief. This grief was a compilation of everything I had been going through at the time: financial worries, familial problems, and health and safety concerns because of Covid.

I went to the restroom about three times to release the grief. After that, I knew that it wouldn't look good for me to keep doing this.

In hindsight, I probably should have left work early. Another factor to consider is that at the time, I still wasn't comfortable grieving in front of others. Alone? Yes. But not in front of other people. At the time, I could count the number of times on one hand that I let it rip in front of my therapist.

I was so happy when I got home from work that day that I didn't know what to do. Within an hour of arriving at home, I started crying again. And then it was time for my therapy session via Zoom.

I probably got five words out of my mouth before I had to stop talking and release the trapped grief that felt more like indigestion at this point. Both my therapist and I knew that it had taken a lot for me to get to this point.

More importantly, when you are in a tremendous amount of pain, sometimes you don't care who is observing you. You just want the pain to end.

In a sense, it makes me think about labor and delivery. As much as you wish you did not have to be in such a vulnerable position, and on display, your desire to get that baby out is more important than people seeing you.

One of the most important things that I can tell you about grief is that it will lessen over time if you 1) allow it to release when it's time, 2) don't give in to the devil telling you that its existence will NEVER end, and 3) give yourself extreme grace and compassion.

The other thing about grief is that there is no right or wrong way to grieve. Your grief journey is designed especially for you. Some people cry. Others shout or yell. Others get it out by serving others. And still others have it to come out in their physical bodies through regurgitation, headaches, body aches, etc.

As the Christians like to say now, "You do you, Boo."

Death.

The last thing that we need in our lives is for someone important to us to die while we are grieving the loss of an important relationship in our life. But it is life. And unfortunately, it happens. And I have experienced it so many times that I have lost count.

No matter how much we try, we cannot control death.

Grief gets complicated when death occurs because you have to take a detour from grieving the relationship that caused your pain to now bringing your attention to the death of your friend or loved one.

God is so intricate in the way that he created us in that once we have grieved a significant amount over this new death, our minds, bodies, and souls automatically know when it's safe to go back to the first relationship that we were grieving, and then you can grieve the two relationships at once.

Trauma.

Experiencing trauma in any shape, form, or fashion can be an obstacle to healing. Why? Trauma impacts us by wounding us emotionally, mentally, spiritually, and physically, and it adds a blurry picture to the events that caused the trauma.

PTSD, and trauma in general, is something that affects millions of people all over the world. The term PTSD itself stands for POST TRAUMATIC STRESS DISORDER. The one thing about PTSD, or any type of trauma, is that you are not immediately aware that this is what is going on. The symptoms are isolated.

It rears its ugly head by attempting to steal our identities. And not only does it attempt to steal our identities, but it also adds an extra layer of mind, body, and soul work than we would normally have if we were just healing from the pain of a relationship.

So then, the underlying question regarding PTSD, or any type of trauma, that an individual experiences, is: What are the symptoms? I am glad that you have asked this question. Some of the symptoms that I have witnessed and/or experienced are, but are not limited to:

- hypervigilance
- violent images, flashbacks, and dreams
- trouble falling and staying asleep
- tachycardia
- arrhythmia
- depression
- black and white thinking
- dissociating
- agoraphobia
- anger and other emotions magnified
- inability to process emotions
- concentration difficulties
- unnatural fear, as if you are on guard for your life
- obtrusive, negative thoughts that are not your own

- amnesia, or blocks of memory missing
- avoidance of places and discussion of traumatic events
- stiffening, folding in, and freezing of the body
- constriction of the stomach
- sense of time gets shifted
- delayed grief
- shutting down
- difficulties conceptualizing how to do something that you might have literally done 100s of times before

When my family first came to Chicago from Memphis, they experienced racism because of the fact that blacks could only hold certain jobs and live in certain areas for fear of corrupting the neighborhoods. This oppression caused a domino effect of even more anger and resentment.

My family suffered from the imprints of PTSD in their DNA from historical, racial, individual, and collective trauma. And then colorism, poverty, and each person's own individual brokenness added another layer of trauma.

Some of the main predictors of PTSD, or any type of trauma that rules our lives, include whether the following is present:

- safety
- predictability
- love
- protection
- a sense of one's own identity

The body has a peculiar way of notifying you when you are overloaded and maxed out from trauma. In the beginning, I had a lot of issues with shallow breathing. This would occur even after walking for only about thirty minutes to and from the grocery store. It literally felt like I was going to run out of air.

Low impact exercises along with deep breathing, and emotionally, mentally, and spiritually healing helped decrease these symptoms.

I made the mistake of going back to work too soon. There were nights when I fell asleep early, but because of the trauma symptoms, I would wake up every forty-five minutes. Other times, I fell asleep at three or four in the morning. That meant that I should have been sleeping until eleven o'clock. However, I had to get up at 6:30 in order to make it to work on time.

At the time, I felt like I had no other choice because of not being paid the correct amount in support money. However, looking back, I know that God would have provided for my kids and I another way in his strength and time, not mine. I learned the hard way that if you don't have your physical health, you can hang it up for trying to work anywhere.

Trauma uses something as simple as the seasons changing to enable you to go back to a traumatic event, making your brain feel the emotions and desires to act like the person you were when the event happened. The truth of the matter is, you are no longer that person.

Whenever this happens, I do the following: remind myself to relax, acknowledge the truth, ground myself in either of my five senses, and let myself know that it is the trauma trying to be in control and take over my identity, and that my identity is in Christ.

I also have to remind myself that it's temporary, even if it lasts for a couple of weeks. Me getting caught up in anxiety when a trauma symptom comes on can be like silly putty in the hands of the Satan.

Trauma does a number when it comes to your sense of time. God says in his word that a thousand years is like one day, and one day like a thousand years. With trauma some life events feel like they happened ten years ago, and others feel like it was just yesterday.

Numbing out is one of the major things that we do when it comes to dealing with trauma. The funny thing about numbing out is that you don't even realize that you are doing it. It is set on automatic.

So, your question may become, if you don't know that you are numbing out, then how can you do something about it? Take a "be still and know" moment. Write down what it is you are doing every day: It could be reading books, cooking food, cleaning, or watching TV.

The next thing to do is to write down how long you are participating in each of these activities. Lastly, think about what happens when these events end, i.e., what emotions come up after reading ten books in a row or binge watching a television show.

You will see that the non-stop Energizer activities you have been doing, whether good or bad, are just another form of numbing out. In order to numb out, you have to basically sign up to go to another world temporarily.

In going to another world, you are in essence escaping your reality, and the truth about the situation you are currently in.

In order to ease up on the numbing out, you have to ease up on the Energizer bunny activities. The feelings will come in. Like an old friend, they will greet you with, "Remember me?"

How Shame Reenforces Trauma

Shame plays a major role in everything. It messes with our identity, self-worth, boundaries, and confidence. As the saying goes, "Shame begets shame begets shame." There are several things that have caused me to feel shame when it comes to trauma.

The first is the shame that I felt because of the aggression that lived in my body from witnessing abuse in my home as a kid. This aggression made me feel impulsive, out of control, and ready to start swinging and punching anything or anyone.

By the grace of God, I never did it. However, the fact that the impulse was there was enough to re-enforce the shame. This aggression did not reduce its intensity until I talked to my therapist about the abuse that I witnessed in my home, along with how my father's absence from the home had affected me in general.

We often think that because a certain situation was for the best, then we can just move on like nothing ever happened.

This is nothing but disillusionment to say the least. Abuse wreaks havoc on our souls, and our souls need to be healed. My soul needed to be healed.

Healed from seeing the wrong portrayal of love. Healed from me being in an emotionally abusive marriage. Healed by a Heavenly Father who is the perfect example of fatherhood. Healed by a God who cared about me as a woman, his daughter, and his child.

The swinging impulse that I speak of is not a done deal. It is contained because of my persistence in carrying around a toolbox with me wherever I go. That toolbox includes therapy, grunts in my throat, kickboxing exercises, and releasing tension through yelling out in the privacy of my own home.

This may seem intense for some. However, when you are eager to live a normal life, you will do what you need to do in order to make that dream a reality.

Witnessing abuse and hearing or watching intense news can trigger my brain to tell my body to store these events as aggression when it is unable to process these events.

Containment does not equal "this will never ever happen again".

This is something I must remind myself from time to time when I get too comfortable, thinking that trauma has completely said goodbye to me.

Another thing that has brought on shame is the fact that my brain is not as sharp as it used to be. There are times when my episodic and sequential memory gets goofed up. It's not like my whole world has ended. But it is just enough to make me feel frustrated.

And when it happens, I know I have to practice mindfulness, deep breathing, and emotional regulation. If I don't, I will start to internalize all the negative impact that trauma has done to my life, and my body in general. And I choose not to operate from this place. I operate from a place of reframing and reclaiming.

I remind myself that I have a choice to feel and process the feelings of inadequacy during those rare times when my brain is off, or I can allow the tape recorder to continue on replay, leading my mind into a downward spiral. I can't do both.

For some reason, we have been trained to think that ignoring our problems is the magic pill to making those problems go away. Ignoring our problems means we are doing alternative construction healing.

The next area that I had to deal with was the shame that had built up in regard to my physical health. Things got so bad, that at one point, I was operating at about 30% capacity. Yes, that is very low. But it was my reality.

Now, I am probably at about eighty percent. I will take the eighty over thirty any day. To soak in the reality of the thirty percent is to face the truth that I was a literal, hot mess that God completely resurrected from the dead.

To soak in the reality of this number is to contemplate the fact that trauma **broke down** my entire immune system, including my adrenal glands, and thyroid.

To soak in this reality is to give myself permission to grieve. Grieve the fact that for four years, the thyroid medication that I had been taking for twenty, stopped taking care of me.

Grieve the fact that tiredness and sleepiness became my companion during this time, and no amount of sleep felt like it was enough. Grieve the fact that I was so sick, that I did not know if I would be around for my children. And lastly, grieve the fact that I was a single parent doing it all on my own, and thinking to myself, "God, why?"

And his response? "Why not?"

Somehow, we think that the extreme hardships and frailties of this world that everyone else has been given, for sure will never come knocking at our door. Until it does. And when it does, we become paralyzed.

Why had my body betrayed me when I needed it most? Why had God betrayed me? God had not betrayed me. I felt like he did because I could not take care of my kids and myself like I used to.

Every now and then, my mind goes back to that place. "What if my thyroid numbers plunge again? What if I experience more trauma? What if I have problems processing when it's time to take an exam? What if. What if. What if. Like my grandmother used to say when I was a kid, " 'If' is a crooked letter."

I can live in fear in regard to my health. But, I choose not to. Fear will eat you alive and attack your nervous system with all its might. Fear will torment you to the point of not being able to sleep at night. And Satan knows it. He will try to take us out any way possible.

For God has not given us a spirit of fear, but of power and of love and of a sound mind. (2 Timothy 1:7, NKJV)

On the other side of that, I have also learned when releasing grief isn't safe when you have trauma/PTSD. Yes, I just mentioned that it is never good to hold it in.

Like in studying English, or any other language, there are always exceptions to the rule. When you are releasing grief, there is a point when you feel grounded, and then there is a point when you know that you are literally freefalling because the grief is trauma-related grief from coming out of dissociation.

Yep. No bottom at all. That is when you pull out. I have learned that if you don't safely pull out, it can cause you to go on a full downward spiral. And that's not good for anyone.

As my therapist helped me to realize, it is non-productive grief at this point. The reason being is that it becomes equivalent to swimming in an emotional sea. No productivity can happen because something has been switched in your body to tell you to grieve everything in your life.

When I pull out of my freefalling state, I also know that one of two things will happen: 1) Either I will return to a normal or more regulatory emotional state, or 2) I will begin to dissociate.

Nine times out of ten, pulling out of a freefalling state will cause dissociation. And then dissociation means the need to ground oneself with one of the five senses. I like to play the follow my finger eye doctor game.

Think of going to the eye doctor. The lights are off, and the eye doctor tells you to follow their finger as they go from left to right, up and down, and then diagonal, with the light shining in your eyes till you think you're going to cry a river. That is how this exercise pretty much works. I understand that what grounds me will be different for what grounds you.

The Thorn and The Gift

I can look at trauma as being both my gift and my thorn in the flesh. It is a thorn in the flesh because sometimes it gets in the way of my thinking and processing, serving as a reminder of what I have been through. Paul could attest to this.

He had a thorn in the flesh that he asked God to remove: *"Even if I should choose to boast, I would not be a fool, because I would be speaking the truth. But I refrain, so no one will think more of me than is warranted by what I do or say, or because of these surpassingly great revelations.*

Therefore, in order to keep me from becoming conceited, I was given a thorn in my flesh, a messenger of Satan, to torment me.

Three times I pleaded with the Lord to take it away from me. But he said to me, "My grace is sufficient for you, for my power is made perfect in weakness." Therefore I will boast all the more gladly about my weaknesses, so that Christ's power may rest on me. That is why, for Christ's sake, I delight in weaknesses, in insults, in hardships, in persecutions, in difficulties. For when I am weak, then I am strong." (2 Corinthians 12: 6-10)

It is a gift in that it has allowed me to be more empathetic and compassionate towards people and their situations. I realize that yes, in God's word we are given the right and wrong ways of living. However, I spent my life in a lot of black and white. Part of it was due to trauma, and the logical, recovering perfectionist in me. The other part was due to the 20-year marriage that I was in, allowing my ex's brokenness of judgmentalism and criticism to become part of my own.

I have learned that there is a lot of gray for why people are who they are, and why they do what they do.

There is not an "a+b=c" equation for life. That is all wishful thinking. Why? We are all broken. We will all make mistakes. We will all need to give and receive grace. You can do all the planning in the world. At the end of the day, God is in control.

The second gift that trauma has given me is that it has allowed me to obtain an increased level of discernment. Curiosity is the first step in going to new levels in our emotional and mental well-being.

"Be still and know" moments allow us to become more aware of the negative and positive energy of others, discerning whether other people are dealing with some sort of trauma themselves, as well as whether or not they pose a risk to us.

It is also a gift because it helps me to remember to never take things for granted. God blessed me with good memory, ability to critically analyze problems and events, and to multitask at a high level. Trauma affected these areas.

There are certain things that have been game changers for me in my healing from trauma, and just life in general. The most valuable asset is walking in the truth. Next to walking in the truth, is to walk in God's love. Love and truth go hand in hand.

In Romans we are told, *"Who shall separate us from the love of Christ? Shall tribulation, or distress, or persecution, or famine, or nakedness, or danger, or sword? As it is written, "For your sake we are being killed all the day long; we are regarded as sheep to be slaughtered.*

No, in all these things we are more than conquerors through him who loved us. For I am sure that neither death nor life, nor angels nor rulers, nor things present nor things to come, nor powers, nor height nor depth, nor anything else in all creation, will be able to separate us from the love of God in Christ Jesus our Lord. (Romans 8:35-39, ESV)

Although my dad's absence was the catalyst to my perfectionism taking root, trauma itself comes with its own built-in coping mechanisms: freeze, fight or flight, and please-appease. The please-appease response to trauma involves seeking the need for approval/validation (perfectionism).

Our wiring often determines the method that we choose as a response to trauma.

This revelation came in the form of a vivid dream, where I was trying so hard to make everything in the house look perfect and running myself ragged with exhaustion and anxiety. I was running around looking like the Energizer Bunny and feeling like I would have a breakdown any minute.

And mind you, this was all in a dream. God told me that he wanted me to be freer than ever. To release the energy and spirit of perfectionism, so that he could take me to higher heights in him.

Where the Spirit of the Lord is, there is freedom. (2 Corinthians 3:17, KJV)

Martha knew a little something about perfectionism. *Luke 10: 38-42* sets the scene of Martha trying to make everything right for Jesus:

"Now it came to pass, as they went, that he entered into a certain village: and a certain woman named Martha received him into her house.

And she had a sister called Mary, which also sat at Jesus' feet, and heard his word. But Martha was cumbered about much serving, and came to him, and said, Lord, dost thou not care that my sister hath left me to serve alone?

Bid her therefore that she help me. And Jesus answered and said unto her, Martha, Martha, thou art careful and troubled about many things: But one thing is needful: and Mary hath chosen that good part, which shall not be taken away from her." (KJV)

Christ was the perfect sacrifice for our sins. When we strive for perfection instead of better, we void out the cause of the cross. It was his perfect love that casted out all fear, even fears of insecurity that drives perfectionism. Perfectionism must thrive off something. And that something is self-condemnation.

Self-condemnation is in direct conflict of Jesus' redemptive work of us on the cross.

"There is therefore now no condemnation to them which are in Christ Jesus, who walk not after the flesh, but after the Spirit. For the law of the Spirit of life in Christ Jesus hath made me free from the law of sin and death.

For what the law could not do, in that it was weak through the flesh, God sending his own Son in the likeness of sinful flesh, and for sin, condemned sin in the flesh: That the righteousness of the law might be fulfilled in us, who walk not after the flesh, but after the Spirit. (Romans 8: 1-4, KJV)

Perfectionism thrives on legalism. *For by grace are ye saved through faith; and that not of yourselves: it is the gift of God: Not of works, lest any man should boast. (Ephesians 2: 8-9, KJV)*

God's grace took care of all our insecurities and brokenness on the cross. This covers all our past, present, and future issues. I praise God that I am now a recovering perfectionist.

It took a long time to get to this point. We cannot fix what we do not know is a problem (sin) in the first place. Once our sin is brought into the light, we must acknowledge our problem. Then, we can go from there.

If there was one thing that I would tell my younger self, it would be, *"Christ is enough"*. In *Galatians 5:1*, Paul tells us, *"Stand fast therefore in the liberty wherewith Christ has made you free and be not entangled again with the yoke of bondage". (KJV)*

"If the Son shall make you free, ye shall be free indeed." (John 8: 32, KJV)

We have the Holy Spirit residing in us, so we can be free. It will not happen in our own power. When we get rid of something, we must replace it with something else.

The opposite of striving is resting. Resting in God. Having God the Father to fill us up with his Living Water and Bread of Life till we overflow with his love and Holy Spirit, and filling the empty void of striving and hustling for crumbs of self-worth is so much more than we could ever ask for.

The Need for a Poison Container

When we think of the word poison, we think of something harmful, or the act of giving something harmful to someone. A container is a type of object that can be used to store or hold something of substance. When we think of the words poison container, a good definition would be an object that contains a harmful substance.

In the case where people are concerned, a poison container would be an individual who serves as another individual's holding tank for all the brokenness that they have, along with the poison that it contains. Another synonym for poison container is punching bag.

Whenever someone inflicts pain upon us, we must have somewhere for it to go. The oppressed person needs somewhere to dump the oppression placed upon them.

There is usually a push/pull that exists where they want you to support them, and at the same time, use you as the container. Unfortunately, people who search for poison containers have not done the hard work of dealing with the trauma that caused the pain in the first place.

When we are sinned against by others, there are three responses that we commonly have to do with the pain:

- We internalize it, and then get it out in a healthy way via therapy, and/or journaling, small group, support group, etc.
- We internalize it, digest it, and transfer it over to self-hate, self-loathing, shame, and depression.

- We dump it onto someone by using them as a poison container.

When option number three is chosen, the first step is to simply find an individual who appears to be "good holding tank" material. These individuals are usually more reserved and appear to be easily controlled.

The problem with looking for the reserved individual is that if this individual has done the work, and have created boundaries for themselves, they are not going to serve as good holding tank material. At one time, I had not done the work.

I had poor boundaries as well. People used me as their poison container all the time. I constantly gave grace until it was cheapened, and I became a doormat.

Now, if there is a situation where I detect that this is happening, I can tell and put a stop to it right away. The healthier we are as individuals, the less of a chance we have of becoming bait.

What God revealed to me through this experience is that anyone can be a person that is filled with poison (undealt with brokenness) from trauma. This means that it could come from overt or covert individuals. We get so used to seeing aggressive personality that we forget that unhealed brokenness can be wrapped up in what appears to be quiet packages.

Some of the things that happen to poison containers are the following:

- Controlling them through any means necessary: anger, meanness, being bossed around, manipulation, and deception.
- A stripping away of their uniqueness/method of doings.
- Changing your name.

- Displaying irritation because of the other person's enjoyment of life and freedom

It is not our responsibility to serve as someone else's poison container. If someone recruits us as their poison container, and we accept the role without any hesitation, it means that something in the relationship is providing a need for us. We may have problems with approval addiction, people pleasing, a rescuer complex, or the need to have some longing filled.

Praise God for his grace, that our trauma and our brokenness do not define us.

God is not done with me yet, and neither is he done with you. We help to eliminate our family's generational sin when we openly confess to God about how broken and sinful that we are, and sincerely ask him to help us change, grow, and give our kids the tools that they need to avoid repeating the cycle.

Post-divorce issues.

Believe it or not, post-divorce issues can be an obstacle to healing. Nine times out of ten, if you were in a toxic relationship, then you are signed up to go back to court post-divorce for several years. I had three years of post-divorce issues. I know some women who have had six to eight.

This process exacerbates, complicates, and prolongs the anger that you have about the marriage or relationship in general. And thus, to be honest, it can make healing a lot harder than it has to be.

Other spin-offs to post-divorce court drama are that of illness and death. Some women have literally finished up the divorce process, and their ex-husband have dropped dead or become ill. In other cases, both parties become ill, which was the case with me and my ex-husband.

In these cases, the more grace and compassion you give yourself, along with having a support system in place, the more you will thrive and heal.

The Naaman Special.

I know you are probably wondering, "What in the world is the Naaman special?" The Naaman special is that you want God to heal you through a prophet or prophetess who places their hands on you and says some words that immediately deliver you from whatever has had you bound.

God still works miracles like this every day. But is that his will for you?

In scripture, Naaman almost missed his blessing of healing from his leprosy because he wanted the prophet to place his hands on him and speak some extraordinary words of God. That's not what God wanted. God wanted Naaman to dip in a dirty river, so to speak, in order to become clean.

"So Naaman came with his horses and with his chariot, and stood at the door of the house of Elisha.

And Elisha sent a messenger unto him, saying, Go and wash in Jordan seven times, and thy flesh shall come again to thee, and thou shalt be clean.

But Naaman was wroth, and went away, and said, Behold, I thought, He will surely come out to me, and stand, and call on the name of the L<small>ORD</small> *his God, and strike his hand over the place, and recover the leper.*

Are not Abana and Pharpar, rivers of Damascus, better than all the waters of Israel? may I not wash in them, and be clean? So he turned and went away in a rage.

And his servants came near, and spake unto him, and said, My father, if the prophet had bid thee do some great thing, wouldest thou not have done it? how much rather then, when he saith to thee, Wash, and be clean?

Then went he down, and dipped himself seven times in Jordan, according to the saying of the man of God: and his flesh came again like unto the flesh of a little child, and he was clean."

(2 Kings 5: 9-14, KJV)

Naaman thought that because of his status, he was exempt from all of that. God loves us. However, he doesn't care what titles we have behind our name. If he is not going to heal us in this "magical" spiritual way, that is his choice. If he blesses someone else to be healed that way, that is also his choice.

Healing is the first thing on the menu. But, unlike Burger King, we can't have it "Our Way". Our method for healing is based upon how we are wired. Some people heal with talk therapy. Others do better with group therapy or healing circles. Still, there are others who heal through art, dancing, or writing therapy. Whatever way is chosen, God will be with us in the fire.

Soul-ties.

The last obstacle that I will discuss is that of a soul-tie. The best way to describe a soul tie is when you are in or have been in a toxic relationship with someone, and that relationship leaves you in a state of craving that person as if you are on drugs. The tripped-out thing about a soul-tie is that you don't realize that it was created until you are leaving the person that the soul-tie was created with.

This was one of the most difficult things that I had to face. I can remember feeling embarrassed to even discuss the issue with my therapist. Her being relaxed about the situation gave me permission to open up and talk about it.

Initially, I subconsciously numbed my entire body so that I would not have to think about it. But remember what we talked about? You cannot heal what you will not feel. I had to feel it.

My therapist encouraged me to allow myself to lean in, press in, and feel. If you never had an idea of how you were affected from the toxic relationship you were in before, add a soul tie onto it and you will find out.

Recovering from a soul tie is like recovering from drug withdrawal, except the drug is the person that you are no longer with. It is important to note that not everyone involved in toxic relationships will end up with a soul tie.

Create An Empowered New Chapter of Life

One of the by-products of reclaiming your power and identity is to create an empowered new chapter of life. To create it, you have to dissect what that really means. To create is to use a form of art to express oneself. To be empowered is to use courage and confidence to make a choice to live by your convictions.

A new chapter is a new start, a new topic or category, a blank slate, if you will. Just like reading a book, new chapters are not exact replicas of previous chapters, although they may be similar.

And then you look at the word "life". I like to think of life as pure evidence of breath and existence. So, creating an empowered new chapter of life would be using an artistic form of courage and confidence to make a choice to live by your convictions by using a blank slate to show pure existence of breath and existence.

Yes, it is a long definition. However, it is what the Holy Spirit gave me. When you create an empowered new chapter of life, you make choices. However, these choices are not made with the old self.

You are making choices with the brand-new self that you have built. This new self is grounded and rooted in your identity and worth in Christ in every area of your life. Everywhere you go, and every relationship that you are involved in, you setup boundaries. Every area means home, work, school, church, ministry, etc.

In our next chapter, we will dissect identity, self-worth, and boundaries.

Identity, Self-Worth, & Boundaries

Identity is a combination of things that make up who we are as a person. These things include your family of origin, the schools you attended, neighborhoods and homes that you lived in, ethnicity, culture, race, socioeconomic status, etc. It is important when it comes to identity that you focus on your being, and not your doing, or profession.

When it comes to identity, we often find ourselves living off the internalized labels that we were given as a kid. The only internalized label that we need is the one that grounds and roots us in Christ.

Think about some flowers that you have in your garden. When you first planted those flowers, you had to make sure that you dug into the dirt deep enough to make sure that the roots of the flowers got deep down in the dirt and attached themselves down below. If you don't, when the storms, wind, and rain come, the flowers are destroyed.

It is the same thing that happens with our identity. Failure to be rooted and grounded deep down in Christ means that when the storms, wind, and rain comes, we are not tossed to and fro, or snatched up by every doctrine and spiritual practice that people bring our way.

Let's read about Samson's identity:

"So he told her everything. "No razor has ever been used on my head," he said, "because I have been a Nazirite dedicated to God from my mother's womb. If my head were shaved, my strength would leave me, and I would become as weak as any other man."

(Judges 16:17, NIV)

Samson relinquished his identity. At what point did you give up yours?

You have to identify the problem in order to figure this one out:

Problem: My machine is broken. I can't do anything. The whole thing is locked up. The slow performance has been building up over time.

Translation:

Problem: I'm broken. I am in a downward spiral of languishing that has been building over time. I'm stuck.

I am often reminded of the lesson that my mom taught me as a kid. She loved me so much that she bought me the things that brought me joy. Some of those things were dolls, their clothes, cars, and accessories.

Whenever she bought me anything, she would say, "Look, these are your _____ that I bought you." She identified those things. Then, she would say, "They cost a lot of money and I want you to take care of them. The way that you treat them, and your home is the way that you teach other people to treat them."

I did not realize it then, but at the time my mother was teaching me a lesson regarding relationships. When we are grounded and rooted in Christ, not in what we do, or who we are with, we place value (worth) on that identity. Then we protect that identity at all costs.

What happens is that we as women have failed to protect our machines (souls), so to speak. We allowed everything and everyone to handle it.

The next thing you have to do is to determine the probable cause:

Is it a hardware, software, virus/malware issue? Is it caused by the end user herself or another end user who has access to this machine?

Translation:

Is it a heart, mind, soul, combo, issue? Is it caused by me or someone else who I am in relationship with?

"But ye are a chosen generation, a royal priesthood, an holy nation, a peculiar people; that ye should shew forth the praises of him who hath called you out of darkness into his marvellous light;"

1 Peter 2:9

Think about what happens when the power goes out in your home. How does it make you feel? How does it make you feel knowing that part of the reason why you are feeling lost, is that part of you were in the darkness of a bad relationship?

God is the God of restoration.

God loved us so much that he adopted us, allowing us to identify ourselves as his sons and daughters, giving us an automatic stamp of approval to our birthright and inheritance.

It is good to know that just like we receive a letter in the mail, along with a key stating that we have been prequalified for a car, Jesus' death on the cross gave us a prequalification stamp of approval with a key to the Kingdom of God before we were even born.

His death on the cross redeemed us. And it brought salvation. We are worthy because of it. We will then in turn have no problem in protecting that royalty by setting up boundaries with how we are treated.

We hear them talk about the royal family on the news all the time. We were already granted our royalty status years ago. And guess what? It did not require approval by the public in case you were wondering.

Worthy means having value, character, wiring, and beliefs that qualifies you for certain treatment. When you know your worth, you won't settle for anything.

"For ye have not received the spirit of bondage again to fear; but ye have received the Spirit of adoption, whereby we cry, Abba, Father."

Romans 8:15

The next questions to ask yourself are:

What jobs does this machine need to perform? How can I make sure that this happens?

Once I understand the end-user, I can place value on this machine as being a necessity for the end-user's productivity, and getting their job done in general.

You are the end-user of your machine (soul).

Because I know my worth in Christ, setting up boundaries becomes a "Have to" instead of a "need to".

After realizing the value of this machine (soul), I need to develop boundaries regarding its usage.

Setup up boundaries for every single relationship that you are in becomes a must.

Creating New Software

The last thing that you must do to reclaim your power and identity is to create new software. That new software is a new mindset. Our minds are the motherboard of our souls.

When the mindset is damaged, everything else is damaged. What happens in the mind controls our emotions and behavior. We cannot have a transformation without renewing our minds. It's just not possible.

Replacing a video card without double checking the motherboard can waste your time and money. Troubleshooting a heart problem for what is really a mindset problem can also drain time and money.

You can't use a machine (PC/soul) if you forget to install the power supply. It is the main power source.

You have to power down to take a break from its resource usage.

Our daily walk with Christ can't be activated without the Holy Spirit. We have to fill up our machines, or we will not power up.

Our minds need an upgrade.

1. **Stop believing the lie that we are powerless.**

Everything we say or do involves a choice. And not making a choice is still making a choice.

2. **State the truth about our circumstances.**

This is the only way that freedom comes. We can't get free from what we won't acknowledge. Remember Fantasy Island? We CANNOT go there if we want to create new software.

3. **You need to feel the feelings, not suppress (stuffing them), ignore, or spiritually bypass them.**

Spiritually bypassing is trying to use scripture to cover up emotional pain. I was the queen of this at first. It was a coping mechanism that I was totally unaware of.

You have to feel in order to heal. Yes, God will be with you in the middle of your mess as you are feeling it. And yes, you need to quote scripture to help remind you he is there. But no, the scripture does not erase emotional pain that must be felt. This is another lie of Satan to prevent us from healing.

God created us very intricately with emotional, mental, spiritual, and physical aspects of our being. Each of these aspects work individually and collectively.

4. **We need to take responsibility for our part.**

As they say, there are two sides to a coin. We have to take responsibility for our side.

No, it isn't your fault that you were sinned against. However, it is your responsibility to now take care of the areas that are broken because of it.

Also, we may have played a part in sinning against the other person in the toxic relationship. We have to take responsibility for that as well.

5. **Admit that you cannot change the past.**

No matter how badly we may want it, we cannot rewrite or revise history. It is a done deal.

Insistence on revising it is insistence on remaining stuck. There are no ifs, ands, or buts about it. You have to admit that what you went through was devastatingly painful and life-altering. And perhaps it was one of worst things that you have experienced.

Even after all of that you cannot change what happened. You have two choices: stay in the would have, should have, could have port, waiting for the ship to come, to turn around and come get you. Or, you can admit what happened, see the lessons that the events/trauma caused you, and move forward. You cannot do both.

6. **Get rid of self-blame and forgive.**

When you get stuck in self-blame, you are judging your old self with old tools, by a new self with new tools. It does not work like that. In this stage, you make peace with the fact that you made the best decision you could have made with the tools and information that you had at the time.

Then you forgive yourself and others so that you can move forward.

7. **Reframe or Remain-The "R or R method"**

What is reframing?

Putting a new frame around an old situation using a new perspective, with the purpose of moving forward.

What is remaining?

Putting an old frame around an old situation using a new perspective, with the purpose of staying stuck.

When you have an old frame in your house that no longer matches the new paint on your wall, you take the painting to the frame shop to have it reframed. It is the same concept when you have a traumatic life event.

The reframe or remain method is not denial or suppression of emotions or truth. It is acknowledging your feelings and making a choice as to whether or not those feelings are going to allow you to remain where you are or move you forward.

Here is an example of this method:

"I acknowledge that what my kids and I went through was painful and traumatic. I am ashamed of the fact that I could not make better decisions for us. I take full responsibility for the fact that I dropped the ball.

However, I made the best decision that I could make with the tools that I had at the time. Now, I can forgive myself, and eliminate self-blame and shame through connection, compassion, and empathy, and move forward, or I can let my past hurts and emotions be my operating system. The choice is mine."

The last part of creating new software is coming up with scripture verses and daily affirmations to keep you going throughout the day. Daily affirmations are like having the cherry on top of a sundae.

By themselves, you become painfully aware of the disconnect between the areas of yourself that are healed and those that are not. Along with healing, they become the light that adds a little bit of sparkle to your day.

Here are my daily affirmations:

1. I am beautiful inside and out.
2. I am worthy.
3. I am loved.
4. I have purpose and value.
5. I am the righteousness of God in Christ.
6. I am the head and not the tail.
7. I am fearfully and wonderfully made.
8. I do not have to make up for other peoples' brokenness.
9. I am enough in Christ.

10. God's validation and approval is the most important.
11. I am redeemed.
12. I am forgiven.
13. I am chosen.
14. I am a child of God.
15. I am the daughter of a King.
16. I am royalty.
17. My identity is in Christ.
18. Success is not defined by what I do.
19. I have already been given my keys to the kingdom.
20. My birthright comes with an inheritance.

Remember: You are Enough. Reclaim Your Power and Identity. Grab Your Keys to the Kingdom and Get Your Inheritance. You Chosen One. Redeemed One. Righteousness of God in Christ.

Daughter of the King. Head and Not the Tail. Child of God. Beloved. Rise up! Stand up! "The Lord is Our Banner!"

Acknowledgments

To God be the glory for giving me the strength and opportunity to write for him once again.

This book would not have been possible without hearing the stories of many women who have been trapped in toxic relationships and taken a leap of courage in reclaiming their power and identity so they will know they are enough.

Check out "The Valley of Grace Podcast"

On iTunes, Spotify, Stitcher, Castos, Google

and Apple Podcast, & YouTube

For more books by Katina Horton,

Head over to <u>https://thevalleyofgrace.com</u>

to purchase the following titles:

ABOUT THE AUTHOR

Katina Horton is a life coach, author, speaker, podcaster, computer technician, and the mother of two young adult children.

Her podcast, "The Valley of Grace Podcast", focuses on helping women reclaim their power and identity so they will know they are enough.

As a coach, she uses the core concepts of troubleshooting your PC (soul), building your PC (soul), and creating new software (mindset) to help women reclaim their power and identity so they will know they are enough, break unhealthy relationship patterns, build resilience and flourish, and create an empowered new chapter of life.

She has written nine books, including The Journey, Surrendered, Simply Grace, Valley of Grace, Coming Out of the Valley, Broken Pieces, My Blackness, DIGGING DEEP DOWN IN THOSE ROOTS, and YOU ARE ENOUGH.

Through speaking, she motivates women using spiritual and spoken word poetry, along with a unique and engaging storytelling style that inspires, motivates, empowers, and impacts the audiences for generations to come.

https://thevalleyofgrace.com

www.ingramcontent.com/pod-product-compliance
Lightning Source LLC
Chambersburg PA
CBHW071400160426
42811CB00115B/2432/J